Saving Animals
from Ourselves

Saving Animals from Ourselves

A Manifesto for Healing the Divine Animal Within

Andrew Harvey *and* Carolyn Baker

SAVING ANIMALS FROM OURSELVES
A MANIFESTO FOR HEALING THE DIVINE ANIMAL WITHIN

iUniverse books may be ordered through booksellers or by contacting:

iUniverse
1663 Liberty Drive
Bloomington, IN 47403
www.iuniverse.com
1-800-Authors (1-800-288-4677)

ISBN: 978-1-5320-7449-3 (sc)
ISBN: 978-1-5320-7450-9 (e)

Print information available on the last page.

iUniverse rev. date: 05/06/2019

CONTENTS

DEDICATION

For Jill Angelo Birnbaum, founder, rescuer, and
pack leader of *The Moon Dog Farm.*

Letaba, first-born son of Marah, the White Lioness born in Bethlehem (South Africa) on Christmas Day 2000. ©Jason A.Turner

In the midst of a global lion crisis that treats Africa's most sacred animals as a killing commodity in cross-border trade, Linda Tucker and her lion ecologist partner, Jason A. Turner, have dedicated their lives to the solution. Against the odds, Linda rescued Marah from Bethlehem, the site of a notorious "canned hunting operation" - where lions were stolen from the wild and bred for the bullet. With Jason's expertize, they returned Marah and her three cubs to their ancestral wilderness lands in a scientific reintroduction program. After together establishing the Global White Lion Protection Trust, a leadership organisation that has been campaigning for their protection, Linda pioneered the StarLion eco-educational program for emerging youth leadership in 2004, which presented to Nelson Mandela in 2007. By 2012, she founded the Academy for LionHearted Leadership™of which Andrew Harvey was a founding faculty member.

www.whitelions.org www.lindatuckerfoundation.org

BE INFORMED

DO NOT SUPPORT any facility that allows petting of lion cubs, as these places are directly or indirectly linked to canned hunting, a now notorious cuddle-and-kill lion industry.

FOREWORD
BY MARC BEKOFF

At a moment in the planet's history when humans are precipitating an unprecedented extinction of species, including our own, Andrew Harvey and Carolyn Baker are exploring the root causes of our disconnection from ourselves, from other living beings, and from the Earth. *Saving Animals From Ourselves* is not yet another litany of the horrors of non-human abuse and neglect, but rather, a holistic inquiry into the causes of our "othering" of the more-than-human world and how we can transform our relationship with the animal within ourselves.

Marrying scientific research and mystical tradition, the authors patiently argue that our treatment of other animals in the modern world stems from the notion, attributed to the eighteenth-century Age of Reason, that the animal is yet another machine, devoid of emotions or even what humans experience as physical pain. As a result, non-humans have been objectified and commodified to suit our needs and desires—a notion fostered by early Christianity with its insistence that the Hebrew bible sanctions absolute dominion by humans over animals and the Earth itself.

Through a variety of practices, both psychological and spiritual, Harvey and Baker assist the reader in cultivating a new consciousness of the divine animal within ourselves and in the external world. It is as if they hold the reader's hand in grieving the loss of reverence for animal wisdom, as well as heralding the joy inherent in celebrating the little-known intelligence of many species and what we can learn from it in order to become more deeply and dynamically human.

The structure of *Saving Animals From Ourselves* originates from the authors' familiarity with indigenous rites of passage in which the initiate holds a vision of how the rite of passage can lead him or her into the fullness of adulthood. With that vision, the initiate then faces an ordeal or descent which if allowed and endured, unfolds into integration and a deep sense of interconnectedness with all of life. As with traditional rites of passage, the book ends on a note of celebration and tribute–homage to several of the most notable heroes and heroines of animal rescue and wellbeing.

Saving Animals From Ourselves is both poetic and illuminating and like its authors, remarkably fierce and tender. It is unique among the torrent of volumes currently cascading from ever-widening discoveries regarding the plight and yet stunning potential of a host of threatened species.

This seminal book is an invitation and an invocation on behalf of the sacredness of all animal beings on Earth in a time of potential extinction. It is also a celebration of what is possible in a world where humans and non-humans desperately need each other.

Marc Bekoff,
Professor emeritus of Ecology and Evolutionary Biology, University of Colorado (Boulder)

Author of numerous books including *The Animals' Agenda: Freedom, Compassion, and Coexistence in the Human Age* (with Jessica Pierce), *Canine Confidential: Why Dogs Do What They Do*, and *Unleashing Your Dog: A Field Guide to Giving Your Canine Companion the Best Life Possible* (with Jessica Pierce)

Andrew Harvey—Chicago, Illinois
Carolyn Baker—Boulder, Colorado

What insights then, about our human psyches appear when we return to Earth, when we remember that we are related to everything that has ever existed, when we reinstall ourselves in a world of spring-summer-fall-winter, volcanoes, storms, surf, bison, mycelium, Moon, falcons, sand dunes, galaxies, and redwood groves? What do we discover about ourselves when we consent again to being human animals—bipedal, omnivorous mammals with distinctive capacities for self-reflexive consciousness, dexterity, imagination, and speech? In what ways will we choose to live when we fully remember the naturalness and ecological necessity of death? Who will we see in the mirror when we face up to the present-day realities of human-caused mass extinction, ecosystem collapse, and climate destabilization? And what mystery journey will unfold when we answer the alluring and dangerous summons now emanating from the human soul, from the dreams of Earth, and from an intelligent, evolving, ensouled Universe?

Beyond insights into the nature of our humanity, what will we discover—or remember—about the most effective methods for cultivating our human wholeness once we liberate psychotherapy, coaching, education, and religion from indoor consulting rooms, classrooms, and churches? What happens when we rewild our techniques and practices for facilitating human development—not by merely getting them out the door and onto the land or waters, but, much more significantly, by fashioning approaches in which our encounters with the other-than-human world are the central features?

Wild Mind: A Field Guide to the Human Psyche[1]
—Bill Plotkin

All creatures are like you—
Allah-Ram
Be kind to them.
—Kabir

INTRODUCTION

*If you talk to the animals they will talk to you and you will
know each other. If you do not talk to them, you will not
know them. And what you do not know, you will fear.
What one fears, one destroys.*
— Chief Dan George

Saving Animals from Ourselves is not yet another exploration of the horrors
we are inflicting on animals; it is a call for a revolution in consciousness,
leading to wise, urgent action on behalf of animals and the creation. Our
deepest heartfelt desire in writing this book is to *liberate* animals and to
learn from them.

This book is based on a belief we both fiercely share: That we are
not separate from the Divine, not separate from other humans, and are
inextricably interconnected with the Earth community, with a responsibility
to protect and to live in humble and grateful harmony with the whole of
creation.

We have dedicated our lives to a revolution of human consciousness
because we believe that the whole human race is now going through a
global dark night whose goal is to birth an embodied, divine humanity.
The new humanity will realize the sacredness of its own animal nature
and through that redemptive recognition, salute and work to honor and
preserve the whole animal creation.

Through our exploration of shamanic and mystical traditions, we have
discovered a three-part initiatory system which will be unfolded in this book.
Any sacred initiatory process must begin first with a glorious and inspiring
vision of what is possible to those who awaken to the Real. The second
essential unfolding is of a descent into the depths of the human shadow and

its devastating effects both on humanity and on creation. This requires the courage that the vision has installed in us, for nothing in this descent can be shirked or scanted. In the third part of the initiation, a marriage between the ecstatic wisdom of the vision and the tragic and searing wisdom of the descent takes place to birth profound spiritual maturity—what Jesus characterized as the marriage of the wisdom of the serpent with the innocence of the dove—to birth a resolute commitment to focused, urgent, compassionate action.

We wish to emphasize that the elimination of any aspect of the initiatory process can only flounder rather than facilitate the rebirth and transformation that lovingly awaits our surrender to its invitation. We also hasten to remind the reader that none of us is alone in the journey. As mystics of all traditions know, the Divine will accompany all sincere initiates and flood them with its grace. And as evolutionary mystics also know, the Divine has willed the birth of an embodied, divine humanity in love with and protective of the natural world. If we continue to embrace the vision while bearing witness to the shadow, the organic union of their opposite energies will emerge to birth in us a new kind of human being, willing and able to co-create with the Divine a new world.

At the beginning of each section of this book, we have given a specific practice for you to engage with in order to prepare your heart and mind for the material in that section. Taking the time to do the practice will strengthen and guide you as you metabolize the material by distancing you from egoic intellectualization and instead drawing you closer to your heart and soul.

As you read this book, we ask you to hold in your heart the love, wisdom, awe, companionship, and compassion you share with and for the animal beings in your life and throughout creation. We ask you also to hold in your heart this portion of an ancient Ojibway prayer:

Oh Divine One, oh Sacred One
Teach us love, compassion, and honor
That we may heal the Earth
And heal each other.[2]

Andrew Harvey—Chicago, Illinois
Carolyn Baker—Boulder, Colorado

The Vision

Adore and love Him with your whole being, and He will reveal to
you that each thing in the universe is a vessel full to the brim with
wisdom and beauty. Each thing He will show you is one drop from
the boundless river of His Infinite Beauty. He will take away the veil
that hides the splendor of each thing that exists, and you will see that
each thing is a hidden treasure because of His divine fullness, and you
will know that each thing has already exploded stilly and silently and
made the earth more brilliant than any heaven. At His summoning,
all things have sprung up and made the earth more magnificent
than an emperor wearing a robe of the most resplendent satin.[3]

— Rumi, from *Light Upon Light*
Translated by Andrew Harvey

A Practice for Holding the Vision

At the beginning of each section of this book, we offer a particular spiritual practice for the reader to engage with in order to enrich and facilitate the reading of that section.

In this first section, *The Vision*, we offer the practice of "Expanding the Circle of Love," adapted from the Jewish tradition.

Let your mind grow peaceful and inspire yourself with these four sublime lines from an anonymous rabbi in the Pirkei Avot[4], a collection of rabbinic sayings compiled between 250–275 CE:

> *Creation is the extension of God.*
> *Creation is God encountered in time and space.*
> *Creation is the infinite in the garb of the finite.*
> *To attend to Creation is to attend to God.*

The Practice of Expanding the Circle of Love

The most important thing about the practice of "expanding the circle of love in your heart," is to let it unfold calmly and thoroughly and at its own pace. So at the very beginning, breathe deeply and focus and calm and steady your mind. Try to let every worry or concern melt away from you and inwardly consecrate yourself to a holy desire to experience fully your interbeing with all things and creatures in the great unity of Divine Consciousness. Ask the Divine in whatever form you love it most to grace you through the practice with a deeper knowledge of your oneness with the entire universe and everything in it, so that you can become, in St. Francis's words, "an instrument of peace."

3

Now imagine that you are seated at the center of a large circle; grouped silently all around you are your parents, relations, and close friends. Conjure them all up, one by one, steadily, precisely, and honestly. Do not mask to yourself the dark or unpleasant aspects of any of their characters; allow yourself to experience each of them in their human fullness, in all the ambiguous richness of their personality. Acknowledge as you do so, the shadows in yourself, your own difficulties of temperament, your own problems. Do so without fear or shame and with a calm, forgiving compassion. As each person comes into your mind, say inwardly, something like, "Let us be one in love!" Try with your whole being to extend to everyone who appears in your mind, love and recognition and forgiveness.

Now slowly and painstakingly, extend the circle to include first your colleagues and coworkers, then your acquaintances, and then everyone you have ever seen or met. All kinds of faces and beings will arise in your heart-mind; welcome them all, try to recognize them all as faces of the One and different faces of your own inmost truth. Sometimes you may find yourself meeting a deep resistance within yourself to welcoming a particular person and acknowledging your oneness-in-God with him or her. Don't mask this resistance; be honest about it, then offer it consciously to the Divine to be transformed into divine detachment. If someone particularly enrages or disturbs you, ask God to see him or her for a moment with God's own unconditional love; even if your feeling for that person does not immediately change. Asking like this again and again will slowly breed in you greater wisdom and help you separate the innate compassion of your enlightened nature from the reactivity of your ego.

Now imagine that your circle widens still farther to include everyone you haven't yet met in your own town or city. Then welcome into the circle everyone in the entire world. At this moment in the practice I find it helpful to remember images I have seen on television of people sick or struggling or reeling from some disaster; immediately, I find my heart opens to embrace them and all those suffering like them.

By this stage of "expanding the circle of love," you have included and symbolically declared your inner oneness with the whole human race.

Now turn the attention of your heart to the animal kingdom. Animals are everywhere abused and tortured by us, used in horrible experiments, slaughtered for the pleasure of our table, treated as fifth-class citizens in a world that many of them have inhabited for a far longer period than ourselves. Coming to embrace the animal kingdom in love is essential in our spiritual journey. How can we work together to try to preserve the planet from environmental holocaust if we do not truly know the presence of Divine Spirit in every deer, tiger, dolphin, and whale?

This part of the meditation can provide a marvelous opportunity to celebrate the diversity of nature. Increasingly, we include in this stage as many as possible of those species that are now endangered, naming them and trying to visualize them clearly in all their force and beauty. I find this stiffens my resolve to fight against environmental degradation by making what is happening directly personal. In every species that is destroyed, a part of each one of us is also destroyed. Doing this part of the meditation with focus and sincerity can help make that not just a concept or a piece of poetry, but a living truth.

You are now surrounded in the circle you have created by everyone in the world and all the world's sentient creatures. Now you must do something very sacred and very important; you must calmly remove yourself from the center of the circle. Choose a being or animal that you want to sit or stand near you and visualize yourself beside that individual or animal in the circle. The center of the circle is now empty. Dedicate this emptiness to God, and as you do so, pray that you will always be aware of what you now know—that you are just one in the vast, interconnected circle of being, permeated by God, that stretches around the universe.

The Jewish sages warn us that at this moment, "if one is really doing the practice seriously, one might experience some fear or panic. To feel one's connection with everything that lives can be shocking, even a menacing experience. All normal boundaries of what you have called your 'self' are threatened, and the pain that all sentient beings endure becomes inescapably vivid to you in all its fierce, and sometimes frightening, particulars. If fears arise, don't be surprised. Know that they are arising because you are coming into contact with the demanding truth of the heart. Dedicated your fears to the Divine, and ask for direct grace to transform them into lasting awareness and passionate and active compassion."

Standing beside the being or animal you have chosen, then, allow yourself time to savor the presence of divine power at the center of the circle and the unshakable holy strength of your link to billions of other beings. Allow your mind and heart time to contemplate as deeply as they can whatever emotions, visionary thoughts, and practical solutions may arise in you. Then with great humility and reverence, imagine your hands raised in prayer, return yourself to the center of the circle, and turn around slowly, bowing in all directions, to all beings.

The person who began the meditation at the center and the one who now returns to the center and bows in all directions are two very different people. You must imagine now that your experience of interconnection and your prayer to have all your fears of inmost intimacy with all beings transformed have changed you completely. You are now a "diamond being," an enlightened lover of God and the creation, one with the One in all its manifestations. Because of the holy power you have gained from meditation and from the direct operation through it of divine grace, you are now able to radiate brilliant white light from your open heart in all the four directions. Think of your heart as a flame-crystal within the larger crystal of your transformed body and let its light flow out vibrantly in all directions—sanctifying, blessing, and helping all beings throughout the cosmos.

Finally, with great joy and gratitude, dedicate everything that you have done and experienced in the meditation to the awakening of all beings to their oneness-in-God. Rest in the serene peace that true love and true knowledge are bringing to you and radiating from you.[5]

CHAPTER 1

Opening to the Initiation

Read this astounding poem by Kabir, the great fifteenth-century Indian mystic. He expresses as no one has ever expressed before or after, the tender glory that infuses heart, mind, soul, and body when we are born as divine human beings into what the Upanishads called "The Real," what Jesus called "Kingdom Consciousness," and what the Kalahari Bushmen proclaim as "the First Creation." Read it slowly with reverence and realize that Kabir is speaking about you as you will be when you have realized through grace the goal of God's evolutionary passion for you.

The Beloved Is In Me

The Beloved is in me, and the Beloved is in you,
As life is hidden in every seed.
So rubble your pride, my friend.
And look for Him within you.

When I sit in the heart of His world
A million suns blaze with light.
A burning blue sea spreads across the sky,
Life's turmoil falls quiet,
All the stains of suffering wash away.

Listen to the unstuck bells and drums!
Love is here; plunge into its rapture!

Rains pour down without water;
Rivers are streams of light.

How could I ever express
How blessed I feel
To revel in such vast ecstasy
In my own body?

This is the music
Of soul and soul meeting,
Of the forgetting of all grief.
This is the music
That transcends all coming and going.[6]

We have decided to follow the glory of Kabir with a contemporary poem written by a female mystic that celebrates the redemption of the animal body in us. This celebration is the gift of the Divine Feminine, the gift we all now need to receive to come into our own fully human divinity. From that humble and passionate realization, we can move to protect the.

The Animal In Me

The fact is actual
I am an animal
Being human is my identity
While the only difference of reality
Is the language! Ah ha! The language!
The language in which we all engage.[7]
~ Silvia Chidi

White animals are appearing in many species all over the Earth to reveal the miraculous heart of nature, guide us back to its redemptive truth, and inspire us to urgent action on behalf of the endangered creation.

— Linda Tucker, founder of the White Lion Trust,
in conversation with Andrew Harvey

The Recent Arrival of White Animals

In *White Spirit Animals: Prophets of Change,* J. Zohara Meyerhoff Hieronimus links modern objective science and ancient traditional shamanic beliefs. She explores the meaning of the numerous births of white animals in recent times and what it might portend for humans:

> The White Spirit Animals, as guardians of animal wisdom, are spoken of by cultures that revere them as being remnants of the Ice Age and each is said to have a special purpose on Earth. For example, White Buffalo is a harbinger of peace and abundance according to many Native American tribes. White Bear, the great Earth healer, teaches us about nurturance and patience. The White Lion is a sign that we are entering the age of the heart, according to the myths and prophecies of Zulu elders in Timbavati, Africa. The White Elephants of India and Thailand remind us, as they do those of Hindu and Buddhist faiths, of the meaning of good fortune, compassion, family, and nurturance. The White Wolf songs heard by plains, desert, and arctic peoples speak to our love of community and of our inbred need to cultivate independence as well.[8]

The author suggests that ". . . we are asked by the animals to protect and bond with nature, to act upon our inner voice, and to perform intentional right action—all of which enables engagement in the purposeful and wise actions of everyone and everything. The message of the animals is simple, 'Improve life around you,' to which I add, 'and the life within us.' Westerners in particular have been focused on impacting the outer world and dominating the landscape. Adopting new ways of relating to the world is our task at hand."[9]

What does this recent appearance of white animal beings actually mean? We believe that above all, these beings are offering themselves and their unity of being as an inspiration to us to unify *our* being. The Divine is speaking out of the heart of nature to bring us back to the heart *in* nature so that, empowered by the living experience of our divine animal, we can ground ourselves in our bodies and lives on the Earth and be channels of transcendent love and justice. They are here to warn and to show the way because they are showing us the path of harmony, interconnection, respect, and embodiment.

White Spirit Animals concludes with a glimpse of the vision we are offering in this book:

> Now we can listen to our animal kin. Now we can hear the howl of wolves across the world drum, the purr of nursing bear cubs, the lion's roar of belonging, the trumpeting elephant announcing her place to all, and the sound of buffalo hooves turning over the soil. This is the call of the wild to all of us. This is the call to find a place of balance within ourselves, where we are at one with nature and where we live in loving communion with all of life, taking part in the blessings of Creation with respect and gratitude. This is the hope of the White Spirit messengers, ambassadors from the animal kingdom, calling us home to celebrate our reunion.[10]

Let us pray together with the African shamanic tradition to the white lions:

Prayer for the White Lions

You are the great beasts of the sun
You are as lovely as blooms that spring from the earth
You as magnificent as the sun at dawn
Oh Lions that are white
Make our hearts as great as yours![11]

Remarkable Animal Stories

In gathering research for this book, we encountered a number of stories about animals that deeply moved us and allowed us to glimpse firsthand the vision we articulate in this chapter. The stories are shared by people alive now whose whole being was profoundly altered by their encounters with animals and in some cases, these encounters compelled them to dedicate their lives to rescuing and caring for animals.

Read them slowly and allow their messages to arise gently and fully in the space of your open heart, inspired by these words of the great German mystic Angelus Silesius:

> There's not a grain of sand
> So insignificant
> Not a point so tiny
> Where the wise don't see
> God blazing totally.[12]

Wolf Pup Teaches Feral Dog About Humans
By Susan Eirich, founder of Earthfire Institute

We got the phone call on a Wednesday. There was this wolf-like animal hanging around the yard of the caller. Stephanie lived in a rural subdivision and was worried about his future. She suspected he would eventually be shot if he was left free. He was young, perhaps 5–6 months old, and apparently very lonely. When she was in the house looking out she could see him approach her two little dogs, trying to play with them. Over time he bonded with them. He slept in the bushes near the house. He would bring toys into the yard—a ball he had found, sticks, inviting them to play. She quite fell in love with him.

Eventually she could sit on the porch and he would still hang around, but catching him was another matter. The sheriff came and tried with no success. He was extremely wary. They were also worried that even if they could catch him, where could he go? As skittish as he was, who would adopt him? Someone suggested Earthfire. Often we get calls about wolves or wolf dogs who turn out to be clearly 100% dogs (once we got a call about a dog that resembled a dachshund). Earthfire co-founder, Jean, and I were skeptical, but said we'd come look at him and suggest ways to help trap him.

We met her in town and drove to her place together. It didn't take long to see him—this was as close to home and family that he had, and he was not leaving the area. As we caught our first glimpse of him Jean and I had the same immediate reaction, and understood Stephanie's refusal to leave him at risk. We experienced an instant, powerful urge to protect. He was very wolf-like in body, movement and behavior. But his face! It was the face of an especially sweet German Shepherd. His eyes had the haunted look of an animal who was deeply torn between fear and need; hope and terror, wanting companionship intensely but afraid to approach. There stood in front of us a being caught between two worlds, wild and human. A being who through no fault of his own had inherited two dispositions: wolf and dog. A being driven to fear humans but driven to approach and love them.

The common thread between all these, that spoke clearly, powerfully, unforgettably, across the species barrier was the desperate need for connection and belonging. It was heart wrenching and poignant, watching him invite the dogs to play and succeeding to some degree; a sort of half family. As he stood there, stock still, looking at us, we could feel it . . . he so wanted to connect to humans, but his wild side wouldn't let him. Confused, conflicted, not just pulled but pulled strongly, in two different directions. Jean and I looked at one another and came to an immediate unspoken consensus. We could not let this sweet and tormented animal be shot.

After much consultation we figured out a way to trap him with as little trauma as possible. After the sheriff debacle Stephanie had the foresight to feed him in a large, open Have-a-Heart trap. He went in easily. With his little dog friend next to him in the van, he took the whole thing with surprising calm.

He now resides at Earthfire next to Nightstar, a rambunctious, vibrant, outgoing wolf puppy completely comfortable with humans (positively enjoying them, as a matter of fact). His first reaction to her was fear. After a few days, tentative curiosity. Smaller and younger than he, she overwhelmed him with her joyous fearless vitality and he growled and cowered. But when wolf pups set out to win over a pack member, they don't give up. She intensely demanded; submitted; cajoled; adored, charmed and invited, absolutely irresistibly. After a few encounters he succumbed completely.

She is now his connection to the world. When we take her out for play time he howls desperately, an emotional mess, as if she is lost forever. Rejoices over the top when she comes back. He watches intently as we play with her and sees she is not afraid. When we let them in together, Jean will enter the enclosure and using Nightstar as an intermediary, play with her as she plays with him, licking and pawing his muzzle, leaping and twirling. Jean cannot touch him directly but indirectly, through the medium of a joyous wolf, he is making inroads. A wolf is helping a "dog" connect with humans.

The story has yet to be written. We named him Hope. He is still very afraid of us. But the other day I came home and found Jean lying in the grass next to his enclosure, just lying there, asking nothing, just being. The wolf pup didn't give up on him. Neither will we.[13]

What the Animals Taught Me
By Stephanie Marohn

What the Animals Taught Me is a collection of stories about rescued farm animals in a shelter in Sonoma County, California, and what these animals can teach us. Each story illuminates how animals can help us see and embrace others as they truly are and reconnect us with the natural world.

Wishing to escape the urban rat race, freelance writer and editor Stephanie Marohn moved to rural northern California in 1993. Life was sweet. She was a busy freelancer. In return for reduced rent, she fed and cared for two horses and a donkey. Her life was full.

And then, more farm animals started to appear: a miniature white horse, a donkey, sheep, chickens, followed by deer and other wildlife. Each one needed sanctuary either from abuse, physical injury, or neglect. Marohn took each animal in and gradually turned her 10-acre spread into an animal sanctuary.

Each chapter of *What the Animals Taught Me* focuses on the story of a particular animal that became part of Marohn's life. She shares what she learned from the sheep she rescued from an animal collector, the abused donkey she helped nurse back to health, and many others to remind us that animals have much to teach us about love, compassion, trust, and so many of the qualities we so often try to cultivate in ourselves.

Unconditional Love Lesson #1: Letting Go of Control

It was twelve years ago that Pegasus began my training in the Way of the Horse and she is still my daily companion on that path. With her, I have learned how to walk the line between confidence and dominance. Like many animal lovers, I had always been reluctant to exert my wishes on the animals under my care. "Who am I to decide what they need to do?" I would say. You might be able to get away with that approach when it comes to a cat or a small dog. So the cat gets up on the table. So the dog doesn't always come right away when called. No big deal when safety isn't involved. But out in the pasture, with large animals who can hurt you, unintentionally or not, you have to step firmly into the leadership role.

With animals, what I had to learn was the difference between domination and wise guidance so I could be comfortable stepping up to the leadership plate. With Pegasus, I discovered that truly wise leadership operates through cooperation and harmony. Over time, I deepened my ability to create this with all the animals in my care.

Sadly, the concept of leading through cooperation and harmony is rare in the equestrian world. Many horse people are all about dominance and rule when it comes to their horses. Recently, I was walking with a friend on a forest trail when a woman in the saddle on an obviously distressed horse came down the trail toward us. The horse was wide-eyed, neighing, dancing sideways, turning, and otherwise attempting to escape the tightly reined-in hold the rider was trying to maintain. As they passed us, the rider whipped the horse's neck with a riding crop. I have always hated cruelty toward animals, and seeing it can send me into fierce rage.

In past years, before the animals opened my heart to all beings, I would probably have yelled at the woman, hotly berating her for her abusive treatment of the horse. In my righteous anger, I failed to see the irony of such a reaction—a person mistreating an animal, me mistreating that person. My heart was as closed to the person as the person was to the animal. In my deep upset over abuse of animals, I withdrew all caring for the human involved. I didn't feel such a person deserved to be treated with respect.

But it was different on the trail that day. As the rider passed us, I sent love to the mare with the fervent prayer that the situation would change for her. I also sent love to the rider because I knew she was the one who needed to change. I have the animals to thank for this being my first and instinctual response. I had fully taken in what they had taught me about unconditional love.

Then the rider pulled the horse up just past us, forced the horse around, and struggled to keep her in place. I approached slowly and asked if I could greet the horse. She nodded and I put a hand out to the mare. The mare was too agitated to interact and I could see her anxiety rising. She was nearly out of her head with it.

I began to talk quietly with the woman. In the conversation that followed, she expressed her frustration that the mare just wanted to get back to the barn and her herd and that she often resisted the woman's commands. The woman was forcing the horse to stand facing back up the trail. She was determined that the horse would give in and relax before she turned her around and let her head for home. There was no way that horse was going to relax under all that anger flowing from the person astride her. I could see the situation was escalating as the angry rider continued to try to regain control and the horse became more upset.

"If you don't mind me asking, what's your ultimate goal here?" I inquired, keeping my voice calm with no note of criticism.

"I win, win, win," she said, without hesitation.

And there is the problem, I thought. But I said, "Have you considered that cooperation might be a better basis for a relationship?"

The woman must have taken that in some, because when I suggested that the situation might change if she dismounted and helped the mare calm down, she did. I was thinking how awful it must be for a horse to have on her back a rider whose motivation is to win, win, win, with no thought of what is good for the horse or how distressing that angry, controlling energy must feel coming through the saddle, the stirrups, the reins, and the riding crop into the horse's body with no means for the horse to escape it aside from throwing the rider. The horse either cared enough about her rider not to do that or had been severely punished for it in the past.

When the woman dismounted, I saw the utter relief in the horse's body. She began to calm immediately. Soon the woman allowed the horse to turn for the walk back to the barn.

Before the woman went, I thanked her for letting me talk with her. I was truly grateful for how open she had been. She didn't know me, but yet she had been willing to listen, even in her own obvious distress. I think she was willing to listen to me because I approached her with caring and compassion, rather than with the need to teach her or berate her. What I felt toward her was real and she could feel it; it wouldn't have worked if I had had rage in my heart, but I had put on a show of compassion. I wanted her to stop sending all that angry energy into the horse, but it would work no better with her than with the horse to get angry and yell at her, be "fakely" nice, or otherwise alienate her with attempts at control. I had to try to elicit her cooperation.

I succeeded to a point, but that woman and her horse stayed on my mind for the rest of that day and days afterward. I thought of all that I could have said, should have said to help her see another way of being with her horse.

This is what I wish I had said: Can any relationship with anybody—animal or human—work when the motivation of one of the members in the relationship is to win, win, win? That motivation is all about controlling the other, rather than considering what is in the other's best interests. How can we feel good about a relationship when we know that the other just wants to win? That kind of win means someone has to lose. For a relationship to thrive, there must be a way for both members to win. And that winning can simply be defined as having found a way to work beautifully together. Cooperation and harmony, not control, is the motivation and the goal.

As I see it, humans' attempts to control arise out of fear and pain or, more accurately, the desire to keep from feeling fear and pain. In the case of the rider on the trail, perhaps she did not know how afraid she was, trying and failing to control this large animal. Anger often covers fear. But the attempt to control another only makes us feel worse, as it further closes our hearts. To open our hearts, we must let go of control, of trying to control others and our circumstances. When we do this, we have taken the first step toward being able to love unconditionally, the ultimate in harmonious relationships. When we love unconditionally, everything just works better.

Loving unconditionally doesn't mean, however, that we have no requirements in our relationships. I needed Pegasus to accept the halter so I could maintain her safety and her health. I needed to find another way besides force to reach that goal. Eliciting her cooperation by learning to speak her language, being clear in my objectives, and coming from a place of love and an open heart was that way. Getting angry at her seeming lack of acquiescence would only have entrenched us in a negative cycle that would have closed both our hearts and created years of problems (the woman on the trail was in such a negative cycle with her horse). At the same time, continuing to cry in the pasture, to fold before the task of building cooperation, would also have stalled (sorry!) our relationship.

Developing cooperation requires creativity. When I visited an animal sanctuary in New Zealand, I looked with wonder at all the animals accompanying the director and me as she showed me around—dogs, cats, chickens, baby goats, even rabbits. I asked how she had gotten the dogs not to chase the other animals. "I made what I was doing much more interesting," she said.

Developing cooperation requires more time than ruling by coercion does, but the rewards are great and ever expanding. You may be quickly able to bend an animal to your will using fear and force, but once you see what horses (or dogs or any other beings) who exist in cooperation with humans rather than under their dominion are like, you will never be tempted to go back to the old way of control. (And after my experience with the rider on the trail, I also can't imagine going back to my old way of raging at someone who is mistreating an animal.) Letting go of the need to dominate allows trust and love to blossom. It is a basic lesson in learning to open the heart and love unconditionally. Loving unconditionally means we do not predicate our love on the other doing what we want. Loving unconditionally means we work together for the highest good of both of us. To enter the realm of unconditional love, we let go of our desire to control, and focus instead on our desire to connect and communicate. And soon, a whole field of flowers is blooming before us.[14]

The Return of The Queen to Her Queendom:
The Story of White Lion, Marah
From the White Lion Trust, founded by Linda Tucker

In 2000, a white cub was born in a hunting camp just outside the town of Bethlehem (South Africa) on Christmas Day.

This baby lioness was regarded as having great sacred significance by African elders.

She was named Marah (meaning "Mother of the Sungod") by preeminent African wise man, *Credo Mutwa*.

Unfortunately, the area surrounding Bethlehem in South Africa was the epicenter of the notorious canned lion hunting industry, now widely known as *"Blood Lions."* Lions were forcibly removed from the wild and bred in extermination camps. Cubs are first offered to local visitors and foreign tourism to be petted for a fee, then later, as tame adults, shot as high income-earning trophies.

NOTE: *Although Bethlehem was one of the very first areas to perpetrate these malpractices, this industry is now a widespread in South Africa.*

Back to 2000: through continual forced removals from their natural endemic habitat into these killing camps as well as zoos and circuses around the globe, White Lions were considered extinct in the wild.

Both Marah's parents had been forcibly removed from their birthland in the wilds of Timbavati. Although golden in color, both carried the White Lion recessive gene. After producing many dozens of golden cubs— Marah's siblings—a snow white cub suddenly appeared.

Because both her parents were removed for only one generation from their endemic habitat, Marah was considered of extremely high genetic integrity. However, it was her adorable nature that captured Linda's heart. Through her studies with African lion shamans, who entrusted her with knowledge of the spiritual and cultural importance of these magnificent creatures regarded as the King of Kings, Linda was well-placed to understand the sacred nature of this *amazing little lioness, Marah.*

Holding Marah in her arms in the middle of the killing camp just one day after her birth, Linda promised she would *dedicate her life to ensuring the freedom of the lioness.* It took years to honor that pledge, while a ruthless, unpoliced commercial industry of petting speed-bred baby cubs continued to grow.

Despite the lies that were disseminated by this captive industry about "saving the species," these hand-raised lions could never hope to return to the wild as their genetics had been so badly impaired through speed-breeding. Their familiarity with humans meant they were regarded as "*dangerous predators*" or "*problem animals*" by nature conservation officials.

Back in December 2000, Linda was instructed by the African elders that it was her life-task to ensure the safety and freedom of this precious lioness, and to return Marah to the land of her birthright, Timbavati, at the very heart of the Kruger to Canyons Biosphere. African elders tell us that Timbavati ("*Tsimba-Vaati*") means the Place where the Star Lions came down.

There is a great mystique associated with the geographical coordinates of Timbavati, which align exactly with the Egyptian Sphinx of Giza (humankind's oldest lion riddle). This fact was first delivered to the world in Linda Tucker's ground-breaking book, *Mystery of the White Lions* (2001).

Timbavati was regarded as a sacred site for many hundreds of years by African kings due to the White Lions' re-occurrence in this specific region.

Linda understood that Timbavati was not only the White Lions' natural endemic habitat, it was also their ancestral kingdom.

Given her rare genetic pedigree, this institution in turn was reluctant to release Marah. They identified her as a prime specimen for captive breeding, and refused to part with her. Once again, Linda and her trusted team of advisors, now led by lion ecologist Jason A. Turner, had to fight for Marah's freedom.

While a legal battle took place over the guardianship of Marah, the beautiful lioness was forced to breed by the zoo. She gave birth to a litter of snow white cubs in the dungeons, out of sight of the public.

The ancestral elders named the cubs *Regeus, Letaba* and *Zihra*, meaning *first ray of sunlight* in three different root languages. Their radiant names were all the more poignant as the cubs themselves were unable to see sunlight from their place of captivity for their first nine months, while Linda and her legal team fought to free them and ensured an interdict allowing Marah to raise her cubs herself without human handling or imprinting. This lack of human contact with the cubs was vital for their re-wilding process.

As for freedom, it was now no longer a battle simply for Marah's release from captivity but also for her three precious cubs. Marah's adorable cubs were her direct lineage—so under no circumstances would Linda and her team abandon them to a lifetime of miserable captivity.

Finally, Linda and her team won the long legal battle. The Madonna-like lioness and her three cubs were flown from the zoo to a safe haven in an undisclosed area. This was only made possible because of the extraordinary love and patronage of Mireille Vince, who was prepared to put up the funding for all four lions.

Since Timbavati is the only endemic birthplace of the White Lions, Linda was committed to returning Marah and her cubs to their natural and spiritual homelands.

The next monumental step was the acquisition of the strategic property identified by African elders as the Sacred Heartland of the White Lions in the Timbavati region, where the White Lions reintroduction to the wilds of their original birthplace could safely take place in a carefully phased long-term scientific program.

At last, Linda and her team's challenging long-term objective is finally achievable, as Marah and her three royal cubs are the first White Lions to set paw back in their White Lion kingdom, the sacred homelands which is their birthright.

Today, there are three prides in the protected area created by the Global White Lion Protection Trust, in the heart of their ancestral homelands, Marah's proud lineage.[15]

The Sacred Hopi Snake Dance

Throughout the 1990s, Carolyn repeatedly journeyed from Northern California to the Hopi Reservation in Northern Arizona where she developed many professional and personal relationships with Hopi individuals. She was particularly moved by the part animals played in Hopi ceremony and spirituality.

The reservation is located in an extremely arid part of the American desert Southwest where water is sacred because it was traditionally crucial for the planting and harvesting of corn, the primary staple of the Hopi people. Ironically, beneath the reservation are numerous natural springs. While few are maintained as carefully in the twenty-first century as they were in previous centuries when the springs were the primary source of water on the reservation, water still plays an important part in reservation life and particularly, of ceremonial life. All Hopi ceremony centers around it.

Many Hopi ceremonies include animals or members of animal clans such as Bear Clan, Rabbit Clan, Butterfly Clan, and Snake Clan. Symbols of animal clans are often incorporated into Hopi ceremonies, but no ceremony incorporating animals is as dramatic as the Hopi Snake Dance.

The Hopi Snake Dance is observed for 16 days in August or the early part of September. Scholars believe that the dance was originally a water ceremony because snakes were the traditional guardians of springs. Today the dance is primarily a rain ceremony because the Hopi regard snakes as their "brothers" and rely on them to carry their prayers for rain to the underworld where they believe the gods and spirits of their ancestors live. But, the tourists who come to see the Snake Dance are usually more interested in the spectacle of it, rather than the belief that it has power to influence the weather.

The dance is performed on the last day of the 16-day celebration. It is performed by members of the Snake and Antelope clans from all three of the Hopi mesas, where the Hopis live. This dance is the grand finale of the 16-days and the start of a new ceremonial season.

Preparations take place during the last 9 days of the period such as making the *pahos* or prayer sticks, designing the sand paintings, and building an altar around the paintings which will include bowls of water from a sacred spring, green corn stalks, and trailing vines of melons and beans which are all symbolic of the rain that is essential for the survival of the Hopi and their crops.

During the last 4 days, the Snake Clan priests leave their villages to gather rattlesnakes often taking young boys with them. Hopi legend says that boys of the Snake Clan capture and handle snakes without fear from the time they are born. They stroke the snakes with a feather to make them straighten out their coils because coiling increases the likelihood that they will strike.

What is essential to understanding the Hopi snake ceremony is the *relationship* which must be developed between the man and boys of the Snake Clan who will handle the snakes during the ceremony. While this relationship has not been scientifically researched, some sort of bond develops between the humans and the snakes.

On the last two mornings of the celebration, foot races are held. The runners streak across the desert and up the steep slopes of the mesa just before sunrise in a symbolic gesture that represents the *Kachinas,* or ancestral spirits, bringing water to the village. The winner of the first race gets a ring and a prayer-plume that he plants in his field to ensure a good crop. The second race winner gets a jar of sacred water which he will also pour over his field to bring rain.

On the day the actual dance is held, the snakes that have been caught by the Snake Clan are washed in a large jar filled with water and herbs and then thrown on a bed of clean sand. Young boys guard the snakes to keep them from escaping. The snakes are gathered up in a huge bag and are carried to the village plaza and placed in a *kisi* or snake-shrine.

The highlight of the Snake Dance Ceremony is when the Snake priests reach into the *kisi* and grab a snake. They carry the snake first in their hands and then in their mouths.

Each priest is accompanied by an attendant who uses a wooden rod to prevent the snake from coiling. As the Snake priest and his assistant dance around the plaza, each is followed by a third man called the "gatherer," whose responsibility it is to make sure that when the time comes for the dancer to drop the snake, it doesn't go into the crowd. So, at just the right moment, the gatherer touches the snake with his feathered wand, drops corn meal on it and catches it behind the head. Then he lays it over his arm and goes after another one.

As many as 50 or 60 small whip-snakes, long bull-snakes, and even rattlesnakes can often be seen curling around the gatherers' arms and necks.

Once the bag of snakes is empty, one of the Snake priests makes a large circle of corn meal on the ground. The gatherers throw all of their snakes into the circle, while the women and girls scatter meal on the wriggling pile of snakes. Then the Snake priests hurry in quickly and scoop up armfuls of snakes and dash out of the plaza.

The Snake priests carry the snakes off to special shrines where they are released so they can carry the prayers for rain from the mouths of the priests to the underworld where the rain gods live.

The dance ends with the drinking of an emetic, which makes the dancers vomit, and this is believed to purge them of any dangerous venom.[16]

What must be noted is that while the dancers drink the emetic, they do so at the very end of the dance, by which time, if they have been bitten earlier in the ceremony, they might already be dead or very ill. Thus, we must return again to the relationship that these dancers have developed with the snake prior to the ceremony. In fact, the Snake Clan dancers believe that the life of the dancer depends on the relationship he has developed with these beings leading up to the snake dance.

Since the invention of modern photography and video recording, many images of the Hopi Snake Dance have been captured both in black and white and in color, documenting the extensive physical contact between the dancers and the snakes. The intimacy that Hopi snake dancers experience with their snakes is stunning and also sacred, symbolic not only of their prayers for rain, but their willingness to sacrifice their own well-being for the well-being of the village.

While Carolyn has never personally witnessed the snake dance, she is acquainted with many Hopi who have experienced it countless times, as well as snake dancers who have themselves participated in the formidable ceremony. Snake dancers readily acknowledge the vulnerability and courage they must demonstrate in participating in the ceremony as well as the tender and respectful relationship they have with their snakes. Rather than egotistically claiming bravery for dancing with snakes in their mouths, they are humbled by the experience and consider themselves sacred servants of the village.

As you sit with these four amazing stories and the story of the Hopi Snake Dance, we invite you to contemplate a sublime poem by Christopher Smart, "For I Will Consider "My Cat Jeoffry." Christopher Smart was a great eccentric mystical poet who lived in the eighteenth century and was a dear friend of Dr. Samuel Johnson. My Cat Jeoffry combines precise, clear observation of cat behavior with a cosmic exaltation at how that behavior manifests and celebrates the life force of the One.

Here is that poem in full. Read it slowly twice, and then to appreciate and embody its precise ecstasy, read it aloud. Something that cannot be put into words will dawn in your expanded heart.

For I Will Consider My Cat Jeoffry

For I will consider my Cat Jeoffry.

For he is the servant of the Living God duly and daily serving him.

For at the first glance of the glory of God in the East he worships in his way.

For this is done by wreathing his body seven times round with elegant quickness.

For then he leaps up to catch the musk, which is the blessing of God upon his prayer.

For he rolls upon prank to work it in.

For having done duty and received blessing he begins to consider himself.

For this he performs in ten degrees.

For first he looks upon his forepaws to see if they are clean.

For secondly he kicks up behind to clear away there.

For thirdly he works it upon stretch with the forepaws extended.

For fourthly he sharpens his paws by wood.

For fifthly he washes himself.

For sixthly he rolls upon wash.

For seventhly he fleas himself, that he may not be interrupted upon the beat.

For eighthly he rubs himself against a post.

For ninthly he looks up for his instructions.

For tenthly he goes in quest of food.

For having consider'd God and himself he will consider his neighbour.

For if he meets another cat he will kiss her in kindness.

For when he takes his prey he plays with it to give it a chance.

For one mouse in seven escapes by his dallying.

For when his day's work is done his business more properly begins.

For he keeps the Lord's watch in the night against the adversary.

For he counteracts the powers of darkness by his electrical skin and glaring eyes.

For he counteracts the Devil, who is death, by brisking about the life.

For in his morning orisons he loves the sun and the sun loves him.

For he is of the tribe of Tiger.

For the Cherub Cat is a term of the Angel Tiger.

For he has the subtlety and hissing of a serpent, which in goodness he suppresses.

For he will not do destruction, if he is well fed, neither will he spit without provocation.

For he purrs in thankfulness, when God tells him he's a good Cat.

For he is an instrument for the children to learn benevolence upon.

For every house is incomplete without him and a blessing is lacking in the spirit.

For the Lord commanded Moses concerning the cats at the departure of the Children of Israel from Egypt.

For every family had one cat at least in the bag.

For the English Cats are the best in Europe.

For he is the cleanest in the use of his forepaws of any quadruped.

For the dexterity of his defense is an instance of the love of God to him exceedingly.

For he is the quickest to his mark of any creature.

For he is tenacious of his point.

For he is a mixture of gravity and waggery.

For he knows that God is his Saviour.

For there is nothing sweeter than his peace when at rest.

For there is nothing brisker than his life when in motion.

For he is of the Lord's poor and so indeed is he called by benevolence perpetually—Poor Jeoffry! poor Jeoffry! the rat has bit thy throat.

For I bless the name of the Lord Jesus that Jeoffry is better.

For the divine spirit comes about his body to sustain it in complete cat.

For his tongue is exceeding pure so that it has in purity what it wants in music.

For he is docile and can learn certain things.

For he can set up with gravity which is patience upon approbation.

For he can fetch and carry, which is patience in employment.

For he can jump over a stick which is patience upon proof positive.

For he can spraggle upon waggle at the word of command.

For he can jump from an eminence into his master's bosom.

For he can catch the cork and toss it again.

For he is hated by the hypocrite and miser.

For the former is afraid of detection.

For the latter refuses the charge.

For he camels his back to bear the first notion of business.

For he is good to think on, if a man would express himself neatly.

For he made a great figure in Egypt for his signal services.

For he killed the Ichneumon-rat very pernicious by land.

For his ears are so acute that they sting again.

For from this proceeds the passing quickness of his attention.

For by stroking of him I have found out electricity.

For I perceived God's light about him both wax and fire.

For the Electrical fire is the spiritual substance, which God sends from heaven to sustain the bodies both of man and beast.

For God has blessed him in the variety of his movements.

For, tho he cannot fly, he is an excellent clamberer.

For his motions upon the face of the earth are more than any other quadruped.

For he can tread to all the measures upon the music.

For he can swim for life.

For he can creep.[17]

With Christopher Smart's exaltation perfuming your being, we invite you to contemplate this excerpt from Andrew's book, *The Direct Path*:

> As the divine light of consciousness works on and clarifies and purifies all your physical senses and divinizes them, the essential glory and beauty of nature will become clearer and clearer, more and more astounding, and more and more revelatory of the glory and beauty of the Divine that is everywhere appearing in and as all things and beings in nature. The mountain reveals itself as divine stability; the waters of the sea as the always-flowing divine power; the tiger as divine strength; the anemone as divine delicacy.
>
> One of the greatest and most reassuring mystical experiences of my recent life was seeing my cat Purrball blazing softly in divine light at the top of the stairs, licking her paws. From the moment I first saw this beautiful tabby sitting resignedly at the back of a cage in the pound, my heart contracted

in love for her. That love grew and grew in the weeks and months that followed; I never knew that I could feel so unconditional a tenderness for any creature. I experienced each moment with her as a direct, almost deranging blessing that I began to know was taking me deeper and deeper into the sacred heart of the Father-Mother. It was as if she were the "worm" on the hook of divine love and that divine love, using her as bait, was drawing me into an ever deeper realization of the holiness of all things. Because I loved my cat so much so suddenly, every animal I saw in the street or on television, even animals that I had before disliked or been afraid of, such as cockroaches, boa constrictors, and alligators, all became not only startlingly beautiful but also profoundly touching. I had known for years about the horrible ways in which we treat animals in slaughterhouses, cosmetic factories, vivisection institutes; I had also known many of the facts about the extermination of animal species that our environmental holocaust is causing. Loving my cat more and more made all these forms of knowledge suddenly inescapably real. Every time I saw an abused animal, I saw the face of my cat in pain; every time I read of the disappearance of a species of fish or insect or bird, I saw her face being wiped out by darkness. I realized that the Divine had given me my cat to open my heart finally to the living horror of what we are doing to animals and the natural world.

At first, the immediacy of such naked knowledge scared me. I believed that a great deal of mystical experience had already opened my heart; I was not prepared for this rending of another veil by love. But as I surrendered more and more not only to loving Purrball but to loving all animals and things in nature, in her and through her, I found that I grew in heartbroken love for all things and beings menaced now by the environmental catastrophe human greed and blindness are engineering, and that from that heartbroken love, came a more and more passionate desire to do everything in my power to help others awaken to what I was being shown. I remembered what the old Indian chief had told me years before at a conference in New York: "When you allow yourself really to fall in love with the world, your whole being becomes full of a mother's passion to protect her children, and a father's hunger to see them safe and strong."

And the moment came when one evening, after I had been down to the fridge to drink some milk, I came back up the stairs to our bedroom and saw my cat at the top of the stairs, surrounded by a nimbus of dazzling, sweet, diamond light. Every aspect of her seemed supernaturally precise in that dazzling light; each whisker, the white under her chin, the shining of her eyes, the "M" mark on her forehead—all were utterly clear; it was as if I had never seen them before, never loved or adored or revered them enough. I realized that if I completely married my body, heart, soul, and mind together, I would see all things with this sacramental passion, burning in the glory of God.[18]

Inspired as we are by the momentous arrival of the white animals, buoyed as we are by the animal stories above, elated by the beauty of "My Cat Jeoffry," we must now prepare ourselves to be taught by animals more palpably and profoundly than we have ever been.

The question then arises, how do we embody most fully and effectively this revolution of consciousness so that we allow the subtle and stunning wisdom of animals to help us accept and celebrate the divine animal within us?

CHAPTER 2

A Revolution in Perception: What Could More Than Human Consciousness Offer Humans?

We come to understand that what is reflected by nature is not just who we are now but also who we could become. And so we begin entering nature as a pilgrim in search of his true home, a wanderer with an intimation of communion, a solitary with a suspicion of salvation.
— Bill Plotkin, *Soulcraft* [19]

A scientist should recognize in his philosophy—as he already recognizes in his propaganda—that for the ultimate justification of his activity, it is necessary to look away from knowledge itself to a striving in man's nature [which is] not to be justified of science or reason, for it is in itself the justification of science, of reason, of art, of conduct.
— Arthur Eddington[20]

No change of scientific mind will go far enough that does not return us to the sacramental vision of nature.
— Theodore Roszak[21]

What evil they contrive, how impiously they prepare to shed human
blood itself, who rip at a calf's throat with a knife and listen unmoved
to its bleating, or can kill a goat to eat, that cries like a child, or
feed on a bird, that they themselves have fed! How far does that fall
short of actual murder? Where does the way lead on from there?
Ovid's *Metamorphoses*[22]

We do not embrace the notion that a species as self-destructive as our
own which has spent the last several centuries raping, plundering, and
pillaging planet Earth can be "saved" or could save the ecosystems that
it is in the process of obliterating. All earthlings are confronted not with
a problem that can be solved, but with a predicament that can only be
responded to. Nevertheless, it may be possible, if we can suspend or recover
from our delusion of human superiority, to preserve or restore some facets
of our planet and become more whole in the process. Every person named
in this book who has developed an enduring relationship with an animal
or animals reports that they have through this become inexplicably more
human and lovingly connected in revelatory ways to the whole creation.
We ourselves could write volumes about how our relationships with our
own animal companions have profoundly changed our lives.

We do not wish to idealize animals and their societies as if they live in
impeccable harmony with one another or suggest that if we simply imitate
their behaviors and social structures, we can create utopia. However, the
time for mindfully considering what we might learn from them that
could alter our relationships with ourselves, with each other, and with the
ecosystems is long overdue, with potentially disastrous consequences if we
do not, humbly and urgently do so.

As we made clear in the first section of this book, there has been over
the last fifty years a momentous scientific revolution in our understanding
of the capacities of animals. We believe strongly that this revolution is
as significant as that in quantum physics and astrophysics that reveals
the universe as a paradoxical dance of light, energy, and matter and
as an interconnected web of relationship. What the revolution in our
understanding of animal consciousness shows us unmistakably is what
mystics and shamans have always known; the entire universe is alive, and
each being is gifted with its own sacred powers to be honored, respected,

and celebrated for their unique contribution to the interconnected, pulsing web of life.

It is time that the findings of this scientific revolution that converges magically on the profoundest discoveries of the mystical traditions, rattle finally and completely the foundations of the false separation between humans and animals. This false separation has been touted both by the patriarchal religions and by a scientific orthodoxy that still continues to ignore its own cutting-edge conclusions. If we wish to survive, we will have to jettison absolutely these visions that have given us unparalleled power but increasingly threaten our hearts and souls, by driving us ever deeper into a desperate, violent, nihilistic isolation.

Animal behavior research scientist, Jonathan Balcombe, writes in the conclusion of his book *Second Nature: The Inner Lives of Animals:*

> As we have seen, fishes and other vertebrate animals have inner lives. As individuals with sensations, perceptions, emotions, and awareness, they experience life. Having the capacity to remember past events, and to anticipate future ones, animals' lives are not merely a series of now-moments; by showing that animals have ambient emotional states, we show that their lives play out like a moving tapestry, and they can go better or worse according to their circumstances. As active participants in dynamic communities teeming with other life forms, animals benefit by being on the ball, and learning from their experiences. Many live in rich social networks, where individuals benefit by forming friendships and by cooperating with others.
>
> These capacities endow animals with interests of their own. They are not just living things: *they are beings with lives.* And that makes all the difference in the world.[23]

Western civilization carries within it a very long and brutal tradition of minimizing animal consciousness at best or demonizing it at worst. During the Middle Ages, animals were often deemed evil or possessed with demonic entities. In the so-called Age of Reason, philosophers such as René Descartes perceived them as machines who lacked thought or feeling.

As Jeffery Sinclair writes in his article "Let Us Now Praise Infamous Animals,":

> So what happened? How did animals come to be viewed as mindless commodities? One explanation is that modernity rudely intruded in the rather frail form of René Descartes. The great Cartesian disconnect not only cleaved mind from body, but also severed humans from the natural world. Descartes postulated that animals were mere physical automatons. They were biological machines whose actions were driven solely by bio-physical instincts. Animals lacked the power of cognition, the ability to think and reason. They had a brain but no mind.[24]

We highly recommend reading the remainder of this article as documented below.

You may think that attitudes have substantially changed, but in many parts of the world these soul-deadening assumptions about animals still hold unquestioned sway. Andrew remembers a talk he gave in a church in Texas where he made a passionate plea to dismantle the concentration camp in which we have placed animals. At the end of his talk a beautifully dressed older woman with bleached blonde hair approached him and said, "I so admired your passion, but why do we need animals?" He stood stunned and aghast at what she had said and at the soul-less way she said it. Such outrage boiled in him that he knew he could not make any reply that would not hurt her heart. So he managed to reply, "Ask your own heart, and you'll find out."

In *Where the Wasteland Ends*, author and professor Theodore Roszak traces the disconnection of Western consciousness from Earth and from Earth-based spirituality into the strange interplay of objectivity and alienation which he calls "Newton's sleep." In the fourth century, according to Roszak—the same century in which Constantine declared Christianity as the official religion of the Roman Empire—in Christianity, nature was essentially pronounced dead and desacralized. Thus, man is "existentially outside nature and only temporarily in residence during his mortal life." Ultimately, this means that "nothing can be held sacred or companionable, (it is) a world disenchanted in root and branch into which man has been intruded like a cosmic freak."[25] Obviously, this perspective profoundly influenced investigative methodology, the essence of which necessitated "distrust of anything impulsive or warmly personal and replacing it with the once-removed and coldly other."[26]

Although the philosophers and scientists of the eighteenth century, who were mesmerized by the notion of the universe as a machine, recognized that nature is filled with motion and growth, they attributed those to nature functioning as a machine. Thus to ask questions of meaning or purpose in nature was to them absurd. A machine is dead and cannot choose a purpose and is waiting to be put to use as man sees fit. In the old world of Gnostic philosophers and pagan shamans, all beings radiated meaning, but for modern science studying animal behavior and even for those studying human behavior, "the natural world dies as it hardens into mechanistic imagery."[27]

Scientific investigation increasingly became objective and utilitarian, its primary concern being: What is the usefulness of this natural object to humans? And as Roszak argues, "Objective knowing is alienated knowing; and alienated knowing is, sooner or later, ecologically disastrous knowing. Before the Earth could become an industrial garbage can, it had to first become a research laboratory."[28]

Eighteenth-century poet and philosopher William Blake wrote:

> Unless the eye catch fire,
> The God will not be seen.
> Unless the ear catch fire
> The God will not be heard.
> Unless the tongue catch fire
> The God will not be named.
> Unless the heart catch fire,
> The God will not be loved.
> Unless the mind catch fire,
> The God will not be known.[29]

Roszak champions what he calls the "rhapsodic intellect" by which he means, "a ready awareness of resonance which never lets an idea or action, an image or natural object stray from its transcendent correspondence. Such an intellect loses none of its precision, need sacrifice none of its analytic edge. But it remembers always and first of all where the language in our heads came from. It remembers the visionary origins of culture when all things were, as they still might be, symbolic doorways opening into the reality that gives meaning."[30]

It is this profound shift in perspective, it is the embracing of the "rhapsodic intellect" that is required for an unimpaired and vibrant investigation of animal behavior and animal consciousness. What is essential in this moment of potential extinction of animals and humans is an abandonment of the objective, utilitarian strategy in the study of animals and the willingness to step into a sacramental, mystical approach in which we dare to ask questions of meaning and purpose regarding their behavior and their very presence on our planet.

It is time to cease using animals for our own ends and open in humble wonder to dimensions of animal consciousness that have the potential to transform human consciousness in revolutionary ways that could still even at this late, tragic moment inspire us to live in dignity, awe, and compassionate service to all that share the miracle of life with us.

The Vast Frontier of Animal Consciousness

Anthropomorphism, the attribution of human qualities to animals, is anathema in Western science. However, more recently, ethologist Frans de Waal writes that "When the lively, penetrating eyes lock with ours and challenge us to reveal who we are, we know right away that we are not looking at a 'mere' animal, but at a creature of considerable intellect with a secure sense of its place in the world. We are meeting a member of the same tailless, flat-chested, long-armed primate family to which we ourselves and only a handful of other species belong. We feel the age-old connection before we can stop to think, as people are wont to do, how different we are."[31]

And naturalist George Page, author of *Inside the Animal Mind*, and producer of the "Nature" television series notes, "We should be careful when we're doing science, but when in the name of science we insist on viewing the wild world with no sense whatsoever of 'connection,' the result is just as unsatisfactory and false as the most farfetched, nineteenth-century tale about the dog who enjoyed the joke."[32]

Until recently, research on animal cognition has been conducted largely from the behaviorist perspective which holds that animal cognition and animal behavior are learned as a result of responses to certain stimuli over time. Thus, the notion of an animal having a "mind" has been deemed "unscientific." George Page argues that "It is true that no one can ever prove that animals have consciousness, no more than I can prove you're not a robot, but to declare today that animals absolutely cannot think or feel is no different from theologians of the Middle Ages testifying that the planet Earth cannot possibly orbit the sun. It is just as unscientific as the anecdotal, anthropomorphic assertion that when his owner leaves him alone in the house for ten hours, Fido gets 'depressed.'"[33]

A preponderance of evidence now suggests that animals can and do carry pain in the form of emotional scars for a lifetime. Jane Goodall, in her work at Gombe in Nigeria, tried to help numerous young chimpanzees overcome the traumatic experiences of their childhood. Jane asks why we shouldn't infer emotion when such an inference seems warranted. George Page notes that "She (Goodall) bases this judgment on almost forty years' experience living with chimpanzees. When one of the chimps at the Gombe center jumps up and down and squeals in apparent pleasure in just the way a human child does, Goodall believes we should conclude that this pleasure is not just 'behavior' but that it is felt as pleasure by the chimpanzees as well. . . . She says bluntly, 'I defy anyone who knows anything about children to watch a small chimpanzee and not realize within a very short space of time that *that* child has exactly the same feelings, emotions, fears, despairs as human infants.'"[34]

Research increasingly makes clear that animals have consciousness. It has to be accepted now as fact that animals feel, as we do, a whole smorgasbord of emotions—fear, anger, grief, and happiness. It has to be accepted as a fact also that consciousness in animals is something akin to, though in many ways different from, our own consciousness. Acknowledging these facts is the beginning of entering into the world of mystical truth.

As the Chandogya Upanishad[35] tells us, "As by knowing one gold nugget, dear one, we come to know all things made out of gold—that they differ only in name and form, while the stuff of which all are made is gold; so through spiritual wisdom, dear one, we come to know that all of life is one."

Page concludes *Inside the Animal Mind* by introducing us to Daniel Dennett, author of *Consciousness Explained* and *Kinds of Minds*. "Dennett argues that although language is the 'royal road' to our knowledge of other human minds—with language, we defeat philosophical solipsism; with language we know that other men and women have minds more or less like our own—but it is a flawed tool for the job of understanding animal minds. We ask questions of the natural world in the only way we can—with our language—and in effect we expect animals to answer with this same language." Page notes Dennett's metaphor for trying to use language to understand animal minds: "When we think and talk and write about animals and their minds, it is like studying poetry through a microscope. The answers will never be totally fulfilling; they may well be misleading, and inevitably, something vital will be lost."[36]

The prevailing perspective of the animal mind in the twentieth century was behaviorism, originating from the research of J. D. Watson and B. F. Skinner. Although the field of cognitive ethology or the study of animal cognition has become a respected discipline, behaviorism is still highly influential. A second major influence in the twentieth century was computer science and "information processing." This perspective assumes that the animal mind is nothing more than what the brain experiences. While it is true that much of human and animal behavior is unconscious information processing, the argument that human or animal thought is "nothing but" information processing is absurd.

Page cites Dennett's argument countering the behaviorist approach:

> He argues the importance of questions such as "Why does the fiddler crab have this one enlarged claw? What does he intend to accomplish with it?" Behaviorists recoil in horror, but in asking such questions we're not necessarily saying that the crab in fact does know why. We address such questions in order to learn answers from evolution. Even the simplest bacterium has its reasons, Dennett writes with his usual wit. It isn't aware of them, true, but for us to ignore these reasons in our investigation is folly.[37]

Animals also have emotions. Jane Goodall asserts this after her many years of living with the chimpanzees at Gombe as does Temple Grandin,

Professor of Animal Sciences at Colorado State University. As an autistic woman, Grandin thinks in pictures, not words, and as a result, may come closer than the rest of us to understanding how animals really see and feel about the world. In her essay, "Thinking Like Animals" in *Intimate Nature: The Bond Between Women and Animals*, she writes, "Autistic emotion may be more like an animal's. Fear is the dominant emotion in both autistic people and prey animals such as deer, cattle, and horses. My emotions are simple and straightforward; like an animal's my emotions are not deep-seated. They may be intense while I am expressing them, but they will subside like an afternoon thunderstorm."[38]

In *Kinds of Minds*, Daniel Dennett notes that the inability to talk does not mean that a being does not have a mind. Talking is not necessary for having a mind. Furthermore, the author emphasizes that, "There is just one family tree, on which all living things that have ever lived on this planet can be found—not just animals but plants and algae and bacteria as well. You share a common ancestor with every chimpanzee, every worm, every blade of grass, every redwood tree."[39]

According to Dennett, it is in the relationship between pain, suffering, and consciousness that we discover the deepest connection with the minds of animals and our own:

> If we are concerned to discover and ameliorate unacknowledged instances of suffering in the world, we need to study creatures' lives, not their brains. What happens in their brains is of course highly relevant as a rich source of evidence about what they are doing and how they do it, but what they are doing is in the end just as visible—to a trained observer—as the activities of plants, mountain streams, or internal combustion engines. If we fail to find suffering in the lives we can see (studying them diligently, using all the methods of science), we can rest assured that there is no invisible suffering somewhere in their brains. If we find suffering, we will recognize it without difficulty. It is all too familiar.[40]

Are We Smart Enough to Know?

Frans de Waal, one of the world's most celebrated and pioneering ethologists, dares to ask what would have been an outrageous question to Descartes or Locke or Marx: "Are we smart enough to know how smart animals are?" We have been brainwashed to downplay animal intelligence and, routinely and thoughtlessly, deny them the capacities that we take for granted in ourselves. Humans have their unique way of processing, organizing, and spreading information, but other species have theirs as well. Only recently has science "become open-minded enough to treat all these different methods with wonder and amazement rather than dismissal and denial."[41] De Waal argues that our very limited ability to enter the inner lives of even other humans, whether foreign or familiar, makes it difficult for us to enter the inner lives of animals.

As an ethologist, de Waal has been studying animals his entire life, and he suggests that instead of testing animals on abilities that *we* are particularly good at, we test them on their specialized skills. "This change in perspective," he writes, "is now feeding the long-overdue recognition that intelligent life is not something we must seek at great expense only in the outer reaches of space. It is abundant here on earth, right underneath our non-prehensile [having a keen mental grasp] noses."[42] After all, Darwin reminded us repeatedly that the mental difference between humans and other animals is one of degree rather than kind.

Scientists over the centuries have reeled in horror at the notion of anthropocentrism or the attribution of human form or behavior to an animal, but de Waal argues that it is not as problematic has we may think. Railing against it in the name of scientific objectivity may hide a pre-Darwinian mindset of discomfort with the possibility of humans as animals. Yet in 2018, we know that more than half of our body is not human because "human cells make up only 43% of the body's total cell count. The rest are microscopic colonists."[43]

In a section of his book entitled "The Hunger Games," de Waal asks:

> Are we open-minded enough to assume that other species
> have a mental life? Are we creative enough to investigate it?
> Can we tease apart the roles of attention, motivation, and

cognition? Those three are involved in everything animals do; hence poor performance can be explained by any one of them. . . . It also takes respect. If we test animals under duress, what can we expect?[44]

A Moratorium on the Human-Centric Approach

Frans de Waal courageously calls us to a new perspective:

> Having escaped the Dark Ages in which animals were mere stimulus-response machines, we are free to contemplate their mental lives. It is a great leap forward, the one that Griffin fought for. But now that animal cognition is an increasingly popular topic, we are still facing the mindset that animal cognition can be only a poor substitute of what we humans have. It can't be truly deep and amazing. Toward the end of a long career, many a scholar cannot resist shining a light on human talents by listing all the things we are capable of and animals not. From the human perspective, these conjectures may make a satisfactory read, but for anyone interested, as I am, in the full spectrum of cognitions on our planet, they come across as a colossal waste of time. What a bizarre animal we are that the only question we can ask in relation to our place in nature is "Mirror, mirror on the wall, who is the smartest of them all?"[45]

De Waal notes that in Jane Goodall's research and writing, her description of life at Gombe indicated that her apes had personalities, emotions, and social agendas. She didn't over-humanize them but revealed them as social agents with names and faces who acted as architects of their own destinies. It has become commonplace in the study of animals to assert that only humans truly understand how cooperation works or how to handle competition and freeloading, assuming that it is based mostly on kinship, yet a host of studies reveals that primates who are complete strangers can be cooperative and engage in mutual aid. Yet, "despite these findings," de Waal points out, the human uniqueness meme keeps stubbornly replicating. Are its proponents oblivious to the rampant, varied, and massive cooperation found in nature?"[46]

It is worth asking why this obliviousness to the findings of science in an age that uncritically worships science, still continues. Could it be that humans will ignore anything that threatens their narcissistic and wholly unscientific belief in human superiority, even when it is becoming starkly clear in every area of human life that clinging to this absurdity ensures our destruction? Isn't this what is also happening in our massive denial of climate change? Could it also be that human beings are unconsciously terrified of the savage heartbreak and searing guilt that would overwhelm them if they dared to awake to the truth of animal sentience and intelligence?

Throughout this book we are offering unarguable examples of animal intelligence. While we are not ethologists or evolutionary biologists, we believe that these examples need to be studied in greater depth. For example, as de Waal points out, "Elephants make sophisticated distinctions regarding potential enemies to the point that they classify our own species based on language, age, and gender. How they do so is not entirely clear, but studies like these are beginning to scratch the surface of one of the most enigmatic minds on the planet."[47]

For decades, ecologist Caitlin O'Connell-Rodwell has been studying elephant communication in Etosha National Park in northern Namibia. A research associate at Stanford University School of Medicine, O'Connell-Rodwell observed that elephants seem to detect vibrations in the ground with their feet and trunk. In one of her videos, we follow O'Connell-Rodwell as she investigates whether elephants can detect and interpret other elephants' calls through the ground. Using amplifiers, speakers, geophones and video cameras, she designs an experiment to test how elephant herds respond to an alarm call that elephants produce to warn others of nearby predators, when it is played back through the ground. Elephants can communicate over long distances using low-frequency sounds that travel both in the air and through the ground. O'Connell-Rodwell and others are studying whether elephants can "hear" and interpret these ground vibrations.[48]

De Waal tells us that:

> Dolphins know one another's calls. This by itself is not so
> special, since we too recognize each other's voices, as do

many other animals. The morphology of the vocal apparatus (mouth, tongue, vocal cords, lung capacity) varies greatly, which allows us to recognize voices by their pitch, loudness, and timbre. We have no trouble hearing the gender and age of a speaker or singer, but we also recognize individual voices. When I sit in my office and hear colleagues talking around the corner, I don't need to see them to know who they are. Dolphins go much further, however. They produce signature whistles, which are high-pitched sounds with a modulation that is unique for each individual. Their structure varies the way ring-tone melodies vary. It is not so much the voice but the melody that marks them.

The deep irony of animals calling one another by name is, of course, that it was once taboo for scientists to name their animals. When Imanishi and his followers started doing so, they were ridiculed, as was Goodall when she gave her chimps names like David Greybeard and Flo. The complaint was that by using names we were humanizing our subjects. We were supposed to keep our distance and stay objective, and to never forget that only humans have names. As it turns out, on this issue some animals may have been ahead of us.[49]

What if we studied animal intelligence *and* emotion in greater depth? What if we did so without the terror of anthropomorphism? What if we enlisted some of the great animal ethologists and rescuers mentioned in this book such as Jane Goodall, Marc Bekoff, Frans de Waal, Linda Tucker, Susan Eirich, Caitlin O'Connell-Rodwell, Daniel Dennett, and more to listen and watch and open to an intelligence as sophisticated and complex as human intelligence? What if we stopped simply proclaiming vaguely that "all life is one" and that there is "no separation," and researched that reality scientifically, and married the most precise discoveries of that research to the most incandescent insights of enlightened shamans and mystics? What if the higher intelligences of certain species, such as dolphins, whales, and elephants, could assist us in alleviating some of our human suffering and inspire us in ways we cannot imagine, to curtail and even transform some of the destruction we continue to visit upon animals, ourselves, and the Earth?

Our Sacred Relationship with Creation

Humanity's greatest mystics reveal to us that the entire universe is a sacred marriage of transcendence and immanence of the Eternal Light that is Being, consciousness, bliss, and the billion forms in all worlds that are emanated from it. They also reveal to us that the universe is an ever-evolving child of this sacred marriage. What this means is that everything that is, is inherently and finally sacred. Angelis Silesius said, "A fly in itself is as sublime as an angel."[50] Nothing is more sacred than anything else because all things are sacred.

Our destiny as a human race is either to embrace this vision and enact it on every level of our world or to die out from our continuing ignorance of it. The marvelous news is that this vision has been preserved at the core of the indigenous traditions and is being comprehensively expressed in Native American Faithkeeper, Oren Lyon's great speech to the UN in 1977, which provides a touchstone for the revolution that is now necessary.[51]

Oren Lyons—Native American Onondaga from an address given to the United Nations in 1977

> Power is not manifested in the human being. True power is in the Creator. If we continue to destroy the source of our lives, then our children will suffer. . . . I must warn you that the Creator made us all equal with one another. And not only human beings, but all life is equal.
>
> The equality of our life is what you must understand and the principles by which you must continue on behalf of the future of this world. Economics and technology may assist you, but they will also destroy you if you do not use the principles of equality. Profit and loss mean nothing to future generations. . . .

I do not see a delegation for the four footed. I see no seat for the eagles. We forget and we consider ourselves superior, but we are after all a mere part of the Creation.

We must continue to understand where we are. We stand between the mountain and the ant, somewhere and there only, as part and parcel of the Creation. It is our responsibility, since we have been given the minds to take care of these things.

The elements and the animals and the birds, they live in a state of grace. They are absolute, they can do no wrong. It is only we, the two leggeds, that can do this.

And when we do this to our brothers, to our own brothers, we do the worst in the eyes of the Creator.

It is easy to be greatly inspired by Oren Lyon's words, but what exactly will this revolution in perception require of us?

1) It will require the cessation of any religion's exclusive claim to possessing the truth and the tuning of all religious dogmas and practices in all religions to the revelations of ancestral indigenous wisdom, and those within the religions themselves that honor the Divine Feminine.

2) It will require a scrapping in every religious and mystical system of any suggestion of human uniqueness and privileged destiny in a return to the knowledge that all life is equal.

3) It will require a complete overhaul of all political and economic systems that do not have at their core a precise sense of accountability to all aspects of the creation, grounded in the revelations of scientific research and those of humanity's most awake shamans and mystics.

4) It will require an overhaul of the educational system to enable human beings to prepare to be the vessels of the revelation of the sacred marriage alongside the urgent establishment of world legislative bodies with the power and prestige of the United

Nations to ensure the rights of every living being and of the creation as a whole.

The other extraordinary and even transfiguring news is that if we surrender to our inherent love for animals and allow ourselves to awaken to their beauty and spiritual radiance, they will reveal to us something that the indigenous traditions and illumined mystics have also discovered: Animals can be our guides on the journey toward radical embodiment. They offer just the kind of full-hearted, alert, and grounded presence that they are inherently masters of and that we so now desperately need in order to be strong and wise and empowered enough to deal with the disaster we've created. The tragedy of the cruelty to animals is compounded and made even more frightening when we begin to understand that they are our greatest guides to what we most need.

We have discovered over the years in our personal relationships with our animal companions, the extent to which they have poured out on us their full-bodied, divine animal love that connects us to everything. They have repeatedly broken our hearts, transported us to inexplicable joy, bruised our egos mightily with their incorrigibility, and humbled us to such an extent that on one level we stand in awe of their psychological and spiritual instruction. Perhaps Eckhart Tolle says it best when he notes that he has had a number of Zen masters—all of them cats.[52]

What might we human beings discover of the creation and of our own latent powers if only we were humble enough to open to and trust in the mystery of the guidance of animals? Wholly (holy?) new forms of knowledge, wholly new forms of adjustment to our environment and to embodied *eros*—wholly new understandings of the interlinked realms of what we normalize as reality could be open to us like a constantly expanding, miraculous fan; and the new divine human would have access not only to the tremendous discoveries of the mature mystical traditions, but perhaps even more miraculous initiations into the full range of animal wisdom. This is the future that a revolution in our understanding of the sacred relationship with animals is offering us at the moment of our greatest dereliction. We stand on the threshold of an unprecedented birth of an embodied divine humanity open to celebrating and learning from other forms of consciousness.

In her 2011 *Orion* magazine article recounting her experiences with Athena the octopus and other octopuses noted in *The Soul of an Octopus*, Sy Montgomery quotes Jennifer Mather, lead author of *Octopus: The Ocean's Intelligent Invertebrate*, which includes observations of octopuses who dismantle Lego sets and open screw-top jars. Co-author Roland Anderson reports that octopuses even learned to open the childproof caps on Extra Strength Tylenol pill bottles—a feat that eludes many humans with university degrees. "I think consciousness comes in different flavors," says Mather. "Some may have consciousness in a way we may not be able to imagine."

To reiterate: The consciousness of certain animals has the potential to engender a transformation of consciousness in us. Whether we study the complex behavior of the octopus or the spirit of cooperation that we see among some animals, such as the flight of birds in harmony—not controlling or touching each other, but flowing together seamlessly, individually, but connected—are we not riveted in awe and buoyant curiosity, perhaps even envious, humbly bowing to what may be possible for our own species?

We know that African Matabele ants dress the wounds of comrades injured during hunting raids and nurse them back to health. "After collecting their wounded from the battlefield and carrying them back home, nest-mates become medics, massing around patients for 'intense licking' of open wounds, according to a study in the journal *Proceedings of the Royal Society of Biological Sciences*. This behavior reduces the fatality rate from about 80 percent of injured soldiers to a mere 10 percent."[53]

A Direct Way of Experiencing Interdependence with Animals

Before we unfold for you our vision of interdependence, we would like to invite you to experience it directly as fully and richly as you can in order to prepare your being for realizations that no words can express. The simplest way of doing this is if you have a companion animal who loves you and is nearby. Approach your beloved with sweet words and loving sounds and your whole being tuned to love. Just see what happens, how your beloved animal will open so completely to you and so radiate toward you such embodied love that you feel everything in life is holy and blessed and profoundly beautiful.

Moments like these reveal the living web of love that lives in all of our bodies when we love simply.

Creating a revolution in our perception may be easier than we think. Perhaps it is more about *allowing* a revolution to occur as we experience firsthand our relationships and the relationships of other humans with animals. By this we do not mean the relationships of torturers with animals, but relationships of humans who have not only opened their hearts to animals, but have opened their minds as they knelt in awe of the wisdom, intelligence, and emotional heterogeneity of the more than human world.

Linda Star Wolf notes in her beautiful book *Spirit of the Wolf,* it is useful to consider the extent to which wolves permeate Celtic, Germanic, Roman, and Japanese lore. Our psychic connection with wolves is ancient, and it seems that the wolf has become a being onto which humanity has projected its deepest admiration as well as its darkest fears. Early on, wolf packs began following human hunting parties, and humans gave them leftovers. Wolves and humans hunted together, but eventually, humans began domesticating wolves which over time evolved into dogs. What began as a relationship of co-existence—since humans could not completely tame wolves—then became a relationship of domination and submission. We would suggest that, in fact, the wolf has come to symbolize the human shadow. In exterminating and excluding this being which represents our darkest fears and our shadow material, we also separate ourselves from the wildness, wisdom, and uncanny leadership that wolf consciousness could offer us. Yet many people in addition to Linda Star Wolf have opened to the wisdom of wolf consciousness and other forms of animal consciousness and have been forever changed as a result.[54]

In *Of Wolves and Men*, Barry Lopez draws upon his own experience of living among both captive and free-ranging wolves and notes the interdependence of the Eskimo people of Alaska with wolves. The Eskimo, Lopez asserts, "probably sees in a way that is more analogous to the way the wolf sees than Western man's way of seeing is."[55] In order to live, both the Eskimo and the wolf must hunt and kill animals. In fact, Lopez emphasizes that hunting is a sacred activity among hunting peoples and the very basis of their social organization. However, the interdependence between the Eskimo and the wolf is greatly facilitated by the native perspective, unlike ours, that humans actually are part of the animal kingdom. Whereas non-native members of industrial growth societies tend to focus on the differences between themselves and animals, the Eskimo, defining themselves as members of the animal kingdom focus on the similarities—a reality that becomes more obvious when we note Native American references to "the fish people," "the bear people," "the wolf people," all of whom Native American's recognize as relatives, not strangers.

"With such a strong sense of the interdependence among all creatures and an acute awareness of the ways in which his own life resembled the wolf's," writes Barry Lopez, ". . . the Indian naturally turned to the wolf as a paradigm—a mirror reflection. . . . To fit into the universe, the Indian had to do two things simultaneously: be strong as an individual, and submerge his personal feelings for the good of the tribe. In the eyes of many Native Americans, no other animal did this as well as the wolf. The wolf fulfilled two roles for the Indian: He was a powerful and mysterious animal . . . and he was a medicine animal identified with a particular individual, tribe, or clan."[56]

For many Native Americans, particularly in ceremony, it is important to call on and experience the energy or power of certain animals. Even though the native person may put on the accoutrements of an animal such as a skin or a claw, doing so is not an attempt to imitate the animal, but to *become* the animal energetically. "It is hard for the Western mind," says Lopez, "to grasp this and to take seriously the notion that an Indian at times could *be* Wolf, could actually participate in the animal's spirit, but this is what happened. It wasn't being *like* a wolf; it was having the mindset of Wolf."[57]

And yet, it seems that from the beginning of man's relationship with wolves, man has made a regular business of killing them in the name of predator control, obtaining fur pelts, gathering scientific data, and of course, winning trophies in big game hunting. Often the killing involved torture, and often they were killed with almost pathological dedication, as if wolves held a kind of ominous archetypal significance that exceeded the notion of "predator control." Lopez names this *theriophobia*, that is, "Fear of the beast as an irrational, violent, insatiable creature. Fear of the projected beast in oneself. The fear is composed of two parts: self-hatred and anxiety over the human loss of inhibitions that are common to other animals who do not rape, murder, and pillage. At the heart of *theriophobia* is the fear of one's own nature. In the headiest manifestations, *theriophobia* is projected onto a single animal, the animal becomes a scapegoat, and it is annihilated."[58]

The hatred has Medieval religious roots: the wolf as the Devil in disguise. The Puritans preached against the wilderness as an insult to the Lord, and the drive to tame the wilderness never let up. The wolf became the symbol of what man wanted to kill in himself and in the world— "memories of one's primitive origins in the wilderness, the remnant of his bestial nature which was all that held him back in America from building the greatest empire on the face of the Earth. . . . The image of the wilderness as a figurative chaos out of which man had to bring order was one firmly embedded in the Western mind; but it was closely linked with a contradictory idea: wilderness as holy retreat, wilderness as towering grandeur, soul-stirring and majestic."[59]

Whereas Lopez shares some aspects of the impact of his relationships with wolves in *Of Wolves and Men*, Stephanie Marohn in *What the Animals Taught Me*, shares more directly and intimately her personal transformation through her relationship with farm animals. Both Lopez and Marohn depart dramatically from the rational, linear paradigm of winning and being in control. We believe that much of the genocide of animals in our time, in addition to insatiable greed and a voracious craving for profit, stems from an attempt to ward off feeling fear, vulnerability, and pain. If we control animals without developing any relationship with them, we need not feel the pain and vulnerability inherent in our own animal nature—a nature systematically rejected and minimized in our culture. If we *do* risk developing deep emotional bonds with animals, our lives will be radically altered, in ways that break our hearts, help us bless and integrate both the fragility and the instinctual wisdom of our animal nature, and resplendently bathe us in inexplicable joy.

Stephanie Marohn's journey of rescuing farm animals became a lifelong process of learning from them, not learning about them. In the beginning of her rescuing efforts, she did not know that she would eventually develop a sanctuary for farm animals, or rather, that such a sanctuary would so profoundly develop her. For example, as she interacted with rescued sheep, she discovered the fallacy of "sheep are stupid" and the basic truth that they have their reasons. "Any behavior I have ever witnessed among the animals under my care," she writes, "has a reason. Sometimes the reason is obvious, and sometimes I have to watch or tune in for a while before I understand."[60] Whereas humans ridicule the "flock mentality" of sheep, the truth is that they have little defense against predators except safety in numbers. The flock is actually a powerful social unit, not a bunch of mindless followers. Would we not, as humans, be doing better as a species if we were as connected with each other as sheep are?

Marohn asserts that opening to intimate relationships with animals will transform who we are because we will deeply feel our own animal essence, and if we feel that essence, "it will become impossible to pour toxic waste into rivers and lakes. If we feel that connection, we cannot allow chickens to live their lives packed together into small cages so we can have a seemingly endless supply of eggs."[61]

Yet our deep bonds with animals are not exclusively emotional. In his book *Dogs That Know When Their Owner Is Coming Home*, British scientist Rupert Sheldrake explains morphic fields and morphic resonance between humans and dogs. "For example," Sheldrake writes, "when a dog is strongly bonded to its owner, this bond persists even when the owner is far away and is, I think, the basis of telepathic communication. I see telepathy as a normal, not paranormal, means of communication between members of animal groups. For example many dogs know when their owners are coming home and start waiting for them by a door or window. My experiments on the subject are described in my book, *Dogs That Know When Their Owners Are Coming Home*. Dogs still know even when people set off at times randomly chosen by the experimenter, and travel in unfamiliar vehicles."[62] Sheldrake has concluded that "there are more inclusive forms of consciousness in the universe than human minds,"[63] a perspective that we also share and on which we will be commenting later in this book.

Stephanie Marohn concludes that for her, creating an external sanctuary for animals taught her how to create an internal sanctuary within. The true meaning of sanctuary, she says, is "a place to feel safe, a place where one can be completely oneself, a place of supported independence, a place to live and die in peace, a place of deep connection on a heart and spirit

level, a place of love, honor, and respect for all beings."[64] Through years
of intimate interaction with animals during their births, deaths, injuries,
trauma, and blissful moments of joy, Marohn experienced in her bones
the essence of the Native American expression *Mitakuye Oyasin* or "all my
relations."

In 2000, Diane Knoll traveled to Patagonia to immerse herself, literally
in the first of what would be many subsequent interactions with the
Southern Right Whales. With a Phi Beta Kappa key, Diane was considered
quite educated by Western standards and yet something more, something
unknown was relentlessly calling to her. What she discovered when she
answered that call into the unknown was the sacred world of nature,
ecstasy, meaning, and wholeness. As it is with most humans, the grandeur
of the whales filled her with awe and some fear as she watched them swim
alongside the boat on which she was sailing. Then repeatedly she witnessed
the breathtaking eruption of the gargantuan beings from beneath the
water and heard and felt the majesty of their sounds and their magnificent
spouting. As the reader accompanies her in the story of her encounters with
whales in *Mysticism and Whales,* we feel their heart-stopping immensity
punctuated with surging discharges of sea spray, but we also are silenced
and humbled by their stillness in the water alongside the boat in moments
of human ceremony on board.

Describing the stillness Knoll writes:

> In the presence of whales a hush falls over people. Sacred
> awe, so profound that it becomes the deepest of meditative
> silence. Even when children are present they intuitively
> drift into the quietest of quiet. We have entered a temple
> of soaring grandeur, into a sacred space that transcends all
> cultures, all language, and all religions. Our hearts, our
> bodies, our thoughts, and voices respond. It is a place of
> "ah" where awe dwells.

> What is it about silence, this sacred hush? In this silence
> there is a soft gentleness. Unconsciousness drifts away and
> one becomes supremely conscious. This is not imposed
> silence that evokes an urge to rebel and make noise, this

is not the cold silence of anger refusing to speak, or the awkward silence of not knowing what to say. It is the silence of reverence.

In this silence, as in all types of meditation, the clutter of life falls away, all of the details and "shoulds," plans and goals dissolve. The whales and the sea absorb them. The sense of internal and external ceases. As the quiet ensues, the mind and body expand, becoming different, somehow more, deeper, wider. We are touching and being touched by awe. In this cathedral of the sea, the awe radiates into exquisite love and we are engulfed in an embrace.[65]

Thomas Berry wrote that "The shamanic personality speaks and understands the language of the various creatures of the Earth. Not only is the shamanic type emerging in our society, but also the shamanic dimension of the psyche itself."[66]

The "shamanic dimension" within us is the animal essence that has never left us and never will leave us. In this chapter we have focused on several individuals who intentionally or serendipitously have experienced that dimension through their connection with animals. Most humans have forgotten the ancient inner shaman within—whom we may access through our engagement with other living beings. Knoll cites Dorothy Maclean, one of the co-founders of Findhorn who taught that "divine intelligence is waiting, waiting for humans to become partners, friends, collaborators in life. A door has been created by the whales. It is a doorway to another space, another time, another reality. They are waiting for us."[67]

Recent research indicates that Orca whales have the capacity to imitate human speech. While their imitations do not sound like humans speaking and are perhaps less clear than the utterances of a parrot, they clearly attempt to mimic human speech. "Our results lend support to the hypothesis that the vocal variants observed in natural populations of this species can be socially learned by imitation. The capacity for vocal imitation shown in this study may scaffold the natural vocal traditions of killer whales in the wild," states a report from the Royal Society of Biological Sciences.[68]

Diane Knoll has made many pilgrimages to Patagonia to experience the whales and concludes her book with a distillation of the journey:

> This beautiful experience which began in the year 2000 became a sacred pilgrimage of healing and the discovery of mystical love. My experience blasted open who I thought I was. Having been told who and how I should be and what I should do by my culture, I did not realize that there was an authentic interior longing to be free. I think this is true for many of us. The absoluteness of society is strong. The whales pierced through that covering with a teaching that I was not alone, I was being guided by the Divine and that within me there is a unique Divine core. I was shown who I was called to be rather than who civilization told me I should be. This was a joyous discovery experienced with the whales and with all of Creation. It is the purpose of a Sacred Encounter.[69]

Naturalist, writer, and documentary film maker Sy Montgomery became deeply curious about the octopus. Her life changed forever as a result of a trip to the New England Aquarium where she met, touched, and fell in love with an octopus named Athena. In *The Soul of an Octopus: A Surprising Exploration into the Wonder of Consciousness,* Montgomery recounts her experience of plunging her arms into the icy water of Athena's tank to make contact, how thrilled she was when her new cephalopod friend firmly grasped her, tasting her skin with some of her 1,600 sensitive and powerful suckers. Montgomery also got to know other octopuses named Octavia, Kali, and Karma, stroking their soft heads and observing their many moods and activities, appreciating each distinctively intelligent, willful, inquisitive, mischievous, and affectionate personality. Montgomery writes that, ". . . Athena was more than an octopus. She was an individual—who I liked very much—and also, possibly a portal. She was leading me to a new way of thinking, of imagining what other minds might be like. And she was enticing me to explore, in a way I had never had before, my own planet—a world of mostly water, which I hardly knew."[70]

"What makes this book unusual," writes Brad Plumer at Vox, "is that Montgomery doesn't try to answer this question by sifting through piles of research. Instead, she . . . listens. She develops extensive relationships with a handful of individual octopuses at the New England Aquarium, each with its own personality, its mundane dramas and tragedies. She records every small moment, treating each octopus like a character in a Jane Austen novel. The effect is wonderful. By the end, it's hard to shake the feeling that these bizarre creatures really do have rich internal lives, even if we still lack the imagination to grasp them entirely."[71]

We must respect not only Montgomery's courage in engaging physically with a creature that has grasping tentacles, can spew blinding ink, and has a potentially deadly bite. How does one feel cuddly with such a being? But what Montgomery reveals is the fact that the octopus is a highly intelligent creature that has more emotional capacity than we might imagine—a creature we can establish a life-changing relationship with if only we listen, watch, overcome our fear, and open widely enough.

Squids, octopuses, and cuttlefishes are among the few animals in the world that can change the color of their skin in the blink of an eye. These cephalopods—a group of mollusks with arms attached to their heads—can change their skin tone to match their surroundings, rendering them nearly invisible, or alternatively give themselves a pattern that makes them stand out.[72]

In addition, octopuses can see with their skin. How is this possible?

In "The Octopus Can See With Its Skin," *Guardian* science writer, Mo Costandi, writes:

> Octopuses are well known for changing the color, patterning, and texture of their skin to blend into their surroundings and send signals to each other, an ability that makes them both the envy of, and inspiration for, army engineers trying to develop cloaking devices. As if that wasn't already impressive enough, research published today in the *Journal of Experimental Biology* shows that octopus skin contains the pigment proteins found in eyes, making it responsive to light.
>
> These clever cephalopods can change color thanks to specialized cells called chromatophores, which are packed in their thousands just beneath the skin surface. Each of these cells contains an elastic sac of pigmented granules

surrounded by a ring of muscle, which relax or contract when commanded by nerves extending directly from the brain, making the color inside more or less visible.

Octopuses are thought to rely mainly on vision to bring about these color changes. Despite apparently being color blind, they use their eyes to detect the color of their surroundings, then relax or contract their chromatophores appropriately, which assume one of three basic pattern templates to camouflage them, all within a fraction of a second. Experiments performed in the 1960s showed that chromatophores respond to light, suggesting that they can be controlled without input from the brain, but nobody had followed this up until now.[73]

In *The Soul of an Octopus*, Sy Montgomery demonstrates the stellar quality we notice in the work of Barry Lopez, Stephanie Marohn, and Diane Knoll: wonder. In fact, curiosity alone is not enough. All great scientists are driven by curiosity, but anyone can be curious. The pivotal issue is: Can we stand in the presence of any living being with awe, with not only respect, but the capacity to bow in reverence to the sacred uniqueness with which it graces creation?

Yet perhaps the most remarkable example of wonder in relation to animals is Jane Goodall, who spent more than 30 years studying chimpanzees in the wilderness of Tanzania. Asked by her mentor, Louis Leakey, to go to Africa to study chimpanzees, she took with her not only scientific curiosity, but a remarkably open heart. Of this she notes, "I feel that there's been a disconnect between this [human] clever brain and the heart. Without the heart to ground it and open it to who we really can be as human beings, the brain is a very dangerous machine."[74]

Jane was a revolutionary in the scientific community. First, she was a woman, and her father and male mentors told her that science was not the proper field of study for women. Moreover, her method was revolutionary in the sense that in her era, scientists studied their subjects from afar and did not generally immerse themselves in their subjects' milieu. Jane established her base camp in Gombe in Tanzania where at the time, women were more welcome than men because Tanzanians had grown wary and suspicious of colonizing white males.

While Jane kept meticulous field notes and revised them every evening, she related to the chimpanzees around her not as "subjects" or "objects," but as living beings with complex emotions and social structures. In the scientific milieu of the 1950s, this notion was a taboo concept. *Anthropomorphism* was the prevailing notion of the time and held that we must not attribute human thoughts and emotions to animals. This perspective was held by behaviorists who argued all behaviors are either reflexes produced by a response to certain stimuli in the environment, or a consequence of that individual being's history, including especially reinforcement and punishment.

Citing Jane Goodall as an example, ecologist Carl Safina writes that, "By banning what was considered anthropomorphic, the behaviorists institutionalized the all-too-human conceit that only humans are conscious and can feel anything. Peculiarly, many behaviorists—who are biologists—ignored the core process of biology. Each newer thing is a slight tweak on something older. Everything humans do and possess came from somewhere. Before humans could be assembled, evolution needed to have most of the parts in stock, and those parts were developed for earlier models. We inherited them."[75]

We frequently hear of the extent to which Jane influenced the lives of the chimpanzees of Gombe, but we rarely hear how they influenced her. Perhaps we need only observe her work and look no further, but had she not gone beyond the sexism and anthropomorphism of her day, we would not know what we know today about chimpanzees, nor would Jane be who she is—not only an activist on behalf of animal well-being, but an activist on behalf of *human* justice and well-being also. "I realized," she says, "if we don't help people to have better lives, we can't even try to save the chimpanzees."[76]

In this chapter we have noted several examples of humans whose lives were profoundly influenced by animals. None had dramatic emotional encounters with animals that allowed them to eventually disregard or minimize those encounters and simply "move on." Rather, their entire lives were radically altered in obvious and subtle ways.

Perhaps the most amazing way that loving an animal can transform you is by birthing you into a completely new knowledge of your own animal body and of your divine body that cradles and protects the Divine Animal in you. Love from an animal opens you to the revelation of all of the forms of love being in you and your essential you containing all of the splendors of inner and outer creation in the One. The farthest exploding supernova and the tiniest frisky flea dancing on the palm of your hand are both in your vast You, your essential You—what the Hindus call the Self and the Christian mystics know as the Inner Christ.

Here is Kabir's sublime and precise celebration of this crucial revelation:

> In this body seven seas, rivers and streams,
> In this body moon and sun, millions of stars,
> In this body lightning flashing, brilliance exploding,
> The unstruck sound roaring, nectar streams downpouring,
> In this body the three worlds, in this body their Creator,
> Kabir says: Listen seekers. In this body, right here
> My own personal eternal teacher.

To experience this normally and to act from this experience is the goal to which humanity is, through unimaginably costly mistakes and ordeals, evolving.

A Taste of the Divine Body

Read the Kabir poem above again, slowly and quietly, daring to awaken the sacred imagination in you that knows the truth that Kabir is revealing. In the first two lines, travel from Kabir's images to embrace all the fullness of all of the created universes. In the second set of two lines, realize that the lightning flashing and brilliance exploding of Kabir is an exact description of a precise inner experience of being one with the archetypal powers of Divine Love. Let the poem continue to implode in you and implode you into its radiant field so you can hear the truth of how in you, right now, live the Creator of all the worlds and all the worlds of transcendence and immanence with all of their bodies, in the radiant depths of your own body. Savor the intimate compassion for all human beings and animals that naturally streams from your awakened Self in a mystery you cannot understand, but can live.

One very simple way of experiencing this beyond even Kabir's words is to sit in silence and open your heart in reverence and humility and profound devotion to the One, to the Mystery, to the Beloved with your whole being—mind, heart, soul, and body, consciously energized and lit up by love. Offer yourself to love in its form of golden, tender fire and imagine your whole being, actively being penetrated by that tender, softly-burning, infinitely-loving, all-pervading golden fire that embraces the highest reaches of your being and the tiniest quark and neutrino dancing in your cells. Rest in that rapture and allow Love to teach you directly in silence.

The Academy-award winning 2017 movie, *The Shape of Water*, suggests a profound theme of the divine animal rippling through our current collective consciousness as film maker Guillermo del Toro depicts a tender and impassioned relationship between a humble deaf woman working as a janitor in a classified government research laboratory and a highly evolved animal being, a research subject, with extraordinarily human qualities. Del Toro presents us with two opposing perspectives: The white, male director of the laboratory who was tasked with directing research on the alien animal being during the Cold War from the perspective of brutally subduing and studying it, and the young woman who became insatiably curious about the bizarre being who was kept in a large tank of water in the laboratory at all times and with whom she eventually fell in love. As the story unfolds, we find ourselves, along with other characters in the movie, ceasing to refer to the being as "it" and gradually thinking of the being as "him." The polarization of the dark masculine perspective of exploitation, domination, and destruction with the innocent, sensuous, open-hearted, young feminine attitude could not be more glaring.

While the take-away's from *The Shape of Water* are myriad, we were riveted by the juxtaposition of the "tortured human animal" in the character of the laboratory director and the young woman who fell in love with the "divine animal" and risked her life to rescue him. We are not suggesting that we literally fall in love with animals or engage in bestiality, but we ask you, dear reader, to open your heart and body, with awe, reverence, respect, and humility to the qualities of animal consciousness that can profoundly transform every aspect of your life and that may offer the potential to transport our own species beyond our tortured human animal consciousness to the divine animal consciousness that the more than human world is waiting to offer us.

Dolphins

What appears to be extraordinary intelligence in dolphins was noted by Diane Knoll but has been confirmed in numerous studies such as noted in a 2003 *Guardian* article, "Why Dolphins Are Deep Thinkers":

To keep track of the many different relationships within a large social group, it helps to have an efficient communication system. Dolphins use a variety of clicks and whistles to keep in touch. Some species have a signature whistle, which, like a name, is a unique sound that allows other dolphins to identify it. Dolphins also communicate using touch and body postures. By human definition, there is currently no evidence that dolphins have a language. But we've barely begun to record all their sounds and body signals let alone try to decipher them. At Kewalo Basin Marine Laboratory in Hawaii, Lou Herman and his team set about testing a dolphin's ability to comprehend our language. They developed a sign language to communicate with the dolphins, and the results were remarkable. Not only do the dolphins understand the meaning of individual words, they also understand the significance of word order in a sentence. (One of their star dolphins, Akeakamai, has learned a vocabulary of more than 60 words and can understand more than 2,000 sentences.) Particularly impressive is the dolphins' relaxed attitude when new sentences are introduced. For example, the dolphins generally responded correctly to "touch the frisbee with your tail and then jump over it." This has the characteristics of true understanding, not rigid training.

Lou Herman and Adam Pack taught the dolphins two further signals. One they called "repeat" and the other "different," which called for a change from the current behavior. The dolphins responded correctly. Another test of awareness comes from mirror experiments. Diana Reiss and her researchers installed mirrors inside New York Aquarium to test whether two bottlenose dolphins were self-aware enough to recognize their reflections. They placed markings in non-toxic black ink on various places of the dolphins' bodies. The dolphins swam to the mirror and exposed the black mark to check it out. They spent more time in front of the mirror after being marked than when they were not marked. The ability to recognize themselves in the mirror suggests self-awareness, a quality previously only seen in people and great apes.[77]

The Greek philosopher Plutarch asserted that the dolphin's pattern of assisting humans in distress indicates that they have some sense of justice and regularly act on it even when their actions are not reciprocal or in response to the kindness of humans. They seem to aid humans simply because they are humans and thus Plutarch even asserted that dolphins display moral behavior.[78]

Domestic Pigs

The intelligence of the domestic pig is also stunning. In a study entitled "Thinking Pigs: An Exploration of the Cognitive Complexity of the Domestic Pig,"[79] in the *International Journal of Comparative Psychology,* Lori Marino and Christina Colvin concluded that research on pigs indicates that:

- They have excellent long-term memories.
- They understand symbolic language.
- They have a sense of time, remember specific episodes in their past, and anticipate future events.
- They are excellent at navigating mazes and other spatial tasks.
- They play creatively.
- They live in complex social communities and easily distinguish other individuals, both pigs and human.
- They have an understanding of the perspective of others as shown in their ability to use tactical deception.
- They are emotional and exhibit empathy.
- They show a form of self-recognition and self-agency in their abilities to manipulate joysticks and use mirrors to find food.
- They have distinct personalities.

Sharks

In "Australian Language Shaped by Sharks," BBC journalist Georgia Kenyon notes that for the aboriginal people of Australia, the tiger shark is a pivotal part of their cosmology. "Tiger sharks are very important in our dreaming," said Aboriginal elder Graham Friday, who is a sea ranger there and one of the few remaining speakers of Yanyuwa language. Some people there still believe the tiger shark is their ancestor, and the Yanyuwa are known for their "tiger shark language," as they have so many words for the sea and shark. The Aboriginal Yanyuwa people believe Australia's Gulf of Carpentaria was created by the tiger shark."

In this culture, Kenyon observes, "Language brings about understanding of the shark. The five different words women and men have for shark show how close a bond Yanyuwa have with the animal. Women's words for the shark describe its nurturing side, as a bringer of food and life, while men's words are more akin to 'creator' or 'ancestor.'"

The Yanyuwa are one of thousands of cultures on Earth who attribute their origin to some aspect of the Earth community. Many of these cultures literally spend lifetimes listening to and lovingly communing with the more than human beings from whom they believe they originated. According to them, they know themselves more intimately because of their intimate relationship with the more than human world.

Elephants

Perhaps the most amazingly intelligent non-human creature on Earth is the elephant. In a 2014 *Scientific American* article, "The Science Is In: Elephants Are Even Smarter Than We Realized," Ferris Jabr writes that:

> Over the years numerous observations of wild elephants suggested that the big-brained beasts were some of the most intelligent animals on the planet. They remembered the locations of water holes hundreds of kilometers apart, returning to them year after year. They fashioned twigs into switches to shoo flies and plugged drinking holes with chewed up balls of bark. They clearly formed strong social bonds and even seemed to mourn their dead (see

"When Animals Mourn" in the July 2013 issue of *Scientific American*). Yet scientists rarely investigated this ostensibly immense intellect in carefully managed experiments. Instead, researchers looking for evidence of exceptional mental aptitude in nonhuman animals first turned to chimpanzees and, later, to brainy birds like ravens, crows and some parrots. Only in the past 10 years have scientists rigorously tested elephant cognition. Again and again these new studies have corroborated what zoologists inferred from behavior in the wild.[80]

Elephants are notorious for their spirit of cooperation and empathy. Jabr notes that "in 2008–2009, Frans de Waal and research partner, Joshua Plotnik teamed up to observe 26 Asian elephants at the Elephant Nature Park in Thailand, looking for signs of what researchers call 'consolation.' Many animals are capable of 'reconciliation'—making up after a tussle. Far fewer animals display true consolation: when a bystander goes out of his or her way to comfort the victim of a fight or an individual that is disturbed for some reason. On dozens of occasions Plotnik and de Waal saw elephants consoling one another. A perturbed elephant often perks up its ears and tail and squeals, roars or trumpets. Over the course of the study, many elephants behaved in this way, because of an altercation, because they were spooked by something—such as a helicopter or dog—or for an unknown cause. When other elephants recognized these signs of anxiety, they rushed to the upset animal's side, chirping softly and stroking their fellow elephant's head and genitals. Sometimes the elephants put their trunks in one another's mouths—a sign of trust because doing so risks being bitten."[81]

When we fully metabolize the astonishing intelligence and emotional lives of elephants and a host of other species, how can we permit trophy hunting, killing them in order to protect livestock, keeping them in zoos, torturing them with heinous research experiments, and slaughtering them for food?

What Animals Can Teach Us

Andrew has studied and translated the being and work of Rumi for 35 years and celebrates Rumi with Jesus and Kabir as the three holy beings who continue to shape his vision of evolutionary love in action. For 30 of those years he accepted unquestioningly the Sufi tradition's belief that Rumi himself was guided by three human beloveds during his journey— first Shams, whom Rumi called "my sun"; then Zarkubi, a goldsmith whose simplicity of being, Rumi celebrated as "my moon"; and finally the young and handsome Husammodin, whom Rumi called "my star."

Then a chance encounter with an old Turkish woman at Rumi's tomb in Konya in 2011 changed everything. Andrew had been meditating by Rumi's tomb—the most magnificent in Islam, covered with a brilliant cloth of silver and gold—for several days. An old woman had sat all that time silently by his side, fingering incessantly a rosary of shining dark beads.

On the day of Rumi's death, December 17, the celebrated Sheb-el-Arus, his marriage day to the eternal Beloved, Andrew at last plucked up his courage to speak to the old woman whose devotion has warmed his heart. He asked, "Why do you love Rumi so?"

She turned to him, smiled serenely, and said nothing. Then abruptly she spoke.

"Do you know who lies with him in that tomb?"

"How can anyone lie there with him? Islamic tradition does not permit anyone or anything to be buried with someone recognized as a saint."

She looked at Andrew ironically and gave a short, soft, mocking laugh.

"Shows how little you know, yet," she said.

"Help me then."

For a while the old woman said nothing and then turned again to him.

"I will tell you a story that my great sheik told me [peace be upon him]. I believe you may be ready to hear it because you love Mevlana. You have been blessed for, as you know by now, Rumi is humanity's supreme prophet and poet of love, the rose of glory of Islam, yes, but also a rose whose perfume is for everyone."

She placed both her hands on her heart as if to contain its passion from spilling out of her body.

"Rumi's whole being was a longing to know and experience love ever more deeply. Because love is infinite, the transformations in and through love are infinite. Rumi knew this, lived this, lives this still in unfolding realms of 'light upon light' that have no end. He has blessed me by showing this, who am just an ordinary, lonely old woman nearing her end. That is why I'm not afraid of death, because as Mevlana said, 'How can the lover ever die?'"

She continued so softly, Andrew had to lean forward to hear her. Because his essential being was this longing to experience love ever more deeply, his work was always created from a living experience of love with another loving being.

"Yes, I said first there was Shams, then there was Zakubi, and then Hussamuddin, the beautiful, drew out the glory of the Mathanabi."

He nodded.

"But there is a final secret you do not know, but which I will give to you, on this holiest of all days for the lovers of the beloved. May it expand your heart. Rumi's final and greatest beloved was not a human being. Not Hussamuddin, not even his son, Sultan Vanad whose humility and wisdom made him sometimes weep with gratitude that he had such a son. It was a cat."

"A cat?"

"Yes, a lovely black and brown female cat. She came into his life mysteriously when he was in his early 60s as he was trying to finish his Mathanabi. This female cat fell totally in love with him and he fell totally in love with her. I believe that this was the last gift of the prophet [peace be upon him] to Rumi for the prophet as you know had a particular tenderness for cats."

She paused and closed her eyes and continued.

"Rumi and his cat were inseparable. She would sleep curled in the sleeve of his nightshirt, nestle and purr in his lap when he taught, curl around his feet when he ate. Hers was the first face he saw when he woke, the last face he saw before he fell asleep. My sheik told me that Rumi loved this cat with an infinite love beyond words, beyond even the capacity of his God-kissed words to express and that is why he never speaks of her and never even attempted to write a poem about her. My sheik said it was his cat's love that took him finally into the mystery where all thought and language fall away into a silence of astounded wonder.

"After all his human beloveds who had given him so much and to whom he had given so much came a cat who opened the last door into love for him, the final door into the room where he became, through their sober blissful love, wholly alive in love, mind, heart, soul and body. How can anyone explain this and yet it is true.

"When Mevlana was leaving his body, his cat was with him nestled against him. At the moment our beloved, the beloved of the heart of the world itself, left, the cat stood up, gave a piercing scream, ran into the next room, hid and was discovered stiff and dead the next day. How could she go on living when the source of her life had gone? How could she bear the loneliness of the brutal world without him? His cat followed him in adoration into eternity where they are playing now around the throne with all the angels lost in rapture at their love. I have been shown this. I am not speaking of what I do not know.

"Then something wonderful happened. Rumi's daughter-in-law who adored Mevlana, was the first to discover the dead cat under a chair covered with a green cloth. Green is the color of the Heart, of the eternal springtime of the Heart. She picked up her body, cradled it like one of her own babies in her arms, and my sheik said, she heard the cat say in perfect aristocratic Persian, 'Bury me with him. I belong to him forever as he belongs to me forever.' At first Mevlana's daughter-in-law was afraid. Such a burial would be, as you said, against all Islamic custom. But then love gave her courage and she insisted that Mevlana's cat should be buried with him. Asked why, she proclaimed, 'My father was a friend to all creation.'"

She paused a long time, tears streaming down her face and then went on, "And that is why in the most magnificent and holy of all tombs, after that of the prophet, the supreme lover of the beloved lives forever with his hands folded forever over the body of his cat pressing her to his heart."

Neither of them could speak. Andrew knew he had been blessed and allowed the blessing to sink deep into his heart and into the cells of his body.

At last the old woman got to her feet and spoke, "There is a message in this story, not only for you, but for all human beings in this terrible time when lovelessness is destroying everything. Let yourself let an animal love you and let yourself love an animal wholly with a whole heart, your whole mind clear of thoughts, your whole body alive with tender love and just see what happens."

"What happens?"

"You arrive here fully and forever, your whole being turned to gold."

The old woman left and Andrew remained, allowing everything he had learned about Rumi up to that moment to dissolve in wonder. As he sat there, he remembered being told by a great Marian mystic that Mary had ended her days on earth living along in a small hut in Ephesus tending a few old donkeys, too old and broken down to work in the farms around. After being told this story, he had had a dream. He was walking up a dusty road in a sunburnt landscape and came to a field with old donkeys grazing on the few clumps of grass left unshriveled by the fierce sun. The door of the simple farmhouse in front of him opened slowly. There in a dirty, worn black dress she stood, the Mother of all of us, of all life, and her infinitely sad and gentle, ancient eyes gazed across the field into his and he heard her voice say softly, "Love animals with my love and my love will love you."

Inspired by this holy old Turkish woman's transmission, let us contemplate at least eight lessons animals can teach us, if we dare to open to them with even a fraction of Rumi's love for his cat and the old Mary's love for her donkey.

1) Animals can teach us radical forgiveness. Many domestic animals demonstrate an attitude of forgiveness toward humans even after being horrifically abused by humans. The American pit bull terrier offers the most stunning example. Rescuers of pit bulls report that in the majority of instances of neglect and abuse, when the human mind reasons that an animal that has experienced such mistreatment should only fight back in hostile rage, the pit bull is gentle, kind, and forgiving and demonstrates a general willingness to remain with humans, even in this situation. It is as if they know how tortured and distressed we are, yet they still have compassion for us.

2) Animals can teach us unconditional love. Their love is a given, and it's not dependent on anything we do or don't do. They love

wholly, innocently, finally, and forever. They demonstrate the clearest signs we could have of what mystics know is the infinite love at the core of the Godhead.

3) Animals can teach us profoundly balanced, tender, and embodied love. Human beings have over sexualized *eros*. Animals guide us into a full-bodied, full-hearted, unpossessive, luminously intelligent and divinely tender *eros* that is at once absolutely spiritual and cellularly radiant. This is embodied, divine love, and it is this kind of love that we find in the most whole and evolved saints such as Rumi and Kabir. We can find it in our amazement and awe at the tabby purring against our chest or the supremely trusting dog lying with its ear against our chest listening to our heartbeat, or in the blue jay singing for us alone on a sun-drenched windowsill, or in a white lion stepping out of the dark bush into moonlit shadow, still and ablaze in majesty.

4) Animals can teach us radical acceptance of the rhythms of life and death, light and dark—that radical acceptance that mystical systems celebrate as the gateway into enlightenment. *Animals are masters of surrender—masters of the secrets of being.* While animals do not long for or welcome death, and generally resist it, they also instinctively know that it is an inherent part of life, and they tend to meet it with fearless grace.

Andrew recalls a life-altering incident when he was 28 and staying in the Ambassador Hotel in New Delhi, India. After breakfast he was starting to go for a walk when he saw a dog being hit by a lorry and crawling with a broken back into a ditch in front of him. The dog was clearly in agony. Andrew ran into the hotel and begged the receptionist to summon an ambulance. The receptionist looked at him as if he were crazy, and said, "Millions of people in this city will go to bed without food tonight. Do you really think anyone has time or energy to care about a dying stray dog?" At that moment Andrew had a choice. He could go back to his room and mourn or go out and sit by the helpless and dying dog and accompany him. He chose to sit down by him, still shaking with grief, but he soon realized that the dog was more concerned about Andrew's nervous anxiety than about his dying. The mangy, rail-thin dog with boils on his legs and stomach, raised his head, looked deep into Andrew's eyes, and continued to communicate to him, as he was dying, what Andrew can only describe as a peace beyond understanding. The only eyes Andrew had ever seen comparable to those luminous, infinitely kind and calm and profoundly accepting eyes, are the eyes of Ramana Maharishi, the great enlightened Hindu who for many in the twentieth century represented the highest enlightened state.

5) Jungian commentator Shamdasini says that Jung saw that one of the crucial tasks of complex psychology is that of "coming into a right relation with the animal. . . . There could be no individuation without establishing a new relation to animals." In fact, Jung made clear that "a critical task of analysis is that of 'becoming animal.'" Jung understood too something of vast significance for us in our journey to purify our shadow of rejection of our animal nature. He understood that in nature the animal is "a well-behaved citizen . . . it does nothing extravagant. Only man is extravagant. So if you assimilate the character of the animal, you become a peculiarly law-abiding citizen." (Corbin book p. 206)

We believe that we must now build on Jung's crucial insights to help birth on the Earth human beings who are whole because they have blessed, embraced, and integrated their animal nature and realized in the deepest sense that this leads, not as the patriarchal traditions have implied to surrender to chaotic instinct, but to a profound alignment with the subtle balancing laws of nature. It is to this new human being that our book is dedicated, for we have experienced with Jung the joy and groundedness that are engendered when the so-called civilized sides of ourselves are married to our own inner divine animal.

6) Animals are natural masters of self-protection and the establishing and guarding of boundaries. Too often patriarchal tradition has

characterized these qualities as blind territorial instinct. In fact, as the indigenous traditions know, such qualities are essential for our full human growth and human survival. Without being constantly attentive to the signals and subtle movements of energy within our animal nature, the naturally dissociated, even hubristic nature of our minds can lead us into the most dangerous situations and the most lethal forms of abuse.

If humanity does not heed the ever-shifting wisdom of its animal nature, it will continue on its disastrous, dissociative fantasy of dominating nature, so ensuring its own destruction and the destruction of a majority of the natural world. If we were fully attuned to our animal nature, would we build monstrous, sterile cities where people live lives of lonely alienation? Would we spend hundreds of billions of dollars on a delusional vision of space travel or of colonizing Mars when our own planet is convulsed in crisis? Would we refuse to listen to the warnings of scientists in their increasingly apocalyptic clarity about climate change? Would we continue to turn a blind eye to the epidemic of child abuse, rape, and the degradation of LGBTQ individuals? Would we blindly worship the potential benefits of artificial intelligence and embrace a world run by robots? Would we allow the continuing genocide of animals if we realized that what we are also killing is an inestimably precious part of ourselves which, when gone, will leave us utterly at the mercy of the madness of our dissociated minds and ravaged hearts?

7) Animals also teach us how to rest in being so as to refuel for becoming. They never waste their energy, and they love silence and contemplation and non-conceptual immersion in the real. This is the state that our various mystical systems struggle against great odds to initiate us into. And all around us if we dare to look, we have masters as great as Jesus or the Buddha showing us how being itself can sustain us, inspire and invigorate us through everything. To reiterate Eckhart Tolle: He has had many Zen masters in the form of cats.

As we navigate the global dark night of all species and struggle against immense odds to live and act from our deepest wisdom, we will need to learn how to rest so as to refuel for what is bound to be a long and grueling journey towards a new world. What better teachers could we have to help us incarnate this marriage of opposites than the animals who do it so effortlessly?

8) Animals can teach us to play. Montaigne wrote in the *Apology for Raymond Sebond*, "When I play with my cat, who knows if I am not a pastime to her, more than she is to me?" Montaigne's own work shows us the delicious freedom that can come to someone eased out of his or her self-seriousness to understand what the greatest mystics know: That in the deepest sense the universe and life are games played by divine reality. As Heraclitus said, "Life is a child playing draughts."[82] And as Kabir wrote, "In the beginning . . . this whole universe is endless dance."[83] The genius for play that animals have can be our most direct guide into this blossoming bliss.

Our Many Forms of Resistance

Andrew sent a draft copy of the eight lessons that animals can teach us to two close friends—a young Maori shaman and a famous American Jungian psychoanalyst. The responses were fascinating, to put it mildly. The Maori shaman wrote back tersely, "Yes, yes, yes—our tribe has always known this. Good thing you lot are catching up. Hooray!" The famous Jungian psychoanalyst wrote, "I am sorry to say, dear one, that what you have written is pure anthropomorphic projection. Back to the drawing board!"

Andrew then sent the psychoanalyst's response back to the Maori shaman. He replied at greater length this time: "I wish I could say I was shocked. The resistances to waking up to what animals truly are and what they can teach us are rampant in nearly every Western intellectual I've ever met, even or perhaps especially in the ones who are most supposedly open to indigenous wisdom. Most Western intellectuals and seekers who think they are open to and instructed in indigenous wisdom—because they have been to a few weekend workshops with would-be shamans and can play around with a few concepts—have hardly begun to metabolize it themselves. The resistance is inseparable from their cultural and spiritual training."

Out of the long discussions that arose from these divergent responses, Andrew and Carolyn created a list of the following seven resistances that they identified in themselves as having been profound blocks to their own awakening to the message they are proposing in this book:

1) Religious arrogance—All religious traditions are biased against animal consciousness.

2) Scientific arrogance—Animals are inferior beings and have no feelings. We should study them only to discover how they can serve us.

3) Technological arrogance—We worship our technological powers which seem to prove our superiority but which have shown clearly the potential to destroy us in every way.

4) Our inherent state of anxious and depressed separation divorces us from the wisdom of being that animals radiate as we give preference to *doing* over *being.*

5) Our terror of love and of the responsibility and protection that arise from it. Our fear of the commitment of receiving the overwhelming love of animals. Our terror of being revealed to ourselves as unloving, disembodied, and dissociated—our terror of having our human fantasy of superiority exposed as the vain delirium that it is and so being compelled to rethink everything about our relationship with the creation.

6) Our fear of silence. Animals communicate largely in silence, non-conceptually. This makes it impossible for us to do what we love to do, which is to create despotic games of power and control through words. So animals challenge our addiction to language as the only way to establish control in our world. Ramana Maharishi said, "Silence is unceasing eloquence." What animals can help us learn is what all mystics know to be essential—how to silence our whole being in Being itself and so be constantly receptive to

the instruction that always is streaming toward us, to what Rilke called, "the news that is always arriving from silence."

The great modern Western shaman and poet, John O'Donohue expresses this perfectly when he writes in his book *Walking in Wonder:*

> I think one of the terribly destructive areas of Western thought is that we have excluded animals from the soul, the awareness and the thought world. I feel that animals are maybe more refined than us, and that part of the recognition and respect for the animal is to acknowledge that they inhabit a different universe from us. . . . Part of the wonder of the human mind is when you look towards animals with respect and reverence, you begin to feel the otherness of the world that they actually carry. It must take immense contemplative discipline to be able to hold a world stirring within you and to have no means to express it because animals in the main are silent, and they don't have access to the paradoxical symbolic nuance of language as we have. So I use the word "contemplative" about them in that sense. For me, they are a source of a great kind of wonder. Now, that doesn't mean that I romanticize them—I was born on a farm, and I know farming very well, and I know the other dark side of the animal world too—but there is something really to be wondered at, at the way that they move and the way that they are. Where I envy animals is that I don't think they are haunted by consciousness in the way that humans are.[84]

7) As part of our addiction to doing, we all create vain fantasies of self-importance, and as anyone who has a deep relationship with an animal knows, being and playfulness threaten to dismantle any false grandeur we ascribe to ourselves. This scares us because we are afraid that if we truly surrender to the mastery of being that animals have and to the joyful playfulness for no reason that bubbles from it, the whole edifice of our false self will begin to

crumble and leave us defenseless in the world lunatic asylum where everyone thinks they're so important.

Bradford Keeney's magnificent *The Bushman Way of Tracking God* makes clear the role teasing and sheer play for the joy of it plays in bushman culture, as a way of keeping everyone, even the most advanced shamans, with their feet firmly on the ground. In this as in so much else, it is the bushmen's keen observation of the ways of animals, coupled with their rugged knowledge of the humbling harshness of their desert surroundings that helps them stay sane, attuned, joyful, and grounded.

Professor of Egyptology, Salima Irkram, notes that from the perspective of the ancient Egyptians, animals were just born as God's creatures and could automatically speak the secret language that gods could understand. So for the Egyptians, animals had much greater proximity to divinity, unlike most religions today in which animals are regarded as lesser human beings. For Egyptians, a specific god animated the animal; it was a reincarnation of that god, and the people could pray to and worship it. The sounds animals made were thought to be the secret language of the gods; thus Egyptians felt they were actually closer to divinity than themselves, and would question animals, through a priest's interpretation, on matters as mundane as inheritance or property.[85]

Jungian analyst James Hillman noted that "wherever you look in polytheistic religions—Egypt, Eskimo, India, Mesopotamia, tribal societies—you find that animals are divinities. They were not representations of gods; they *were* gods. Animals were gods because they were eternal . . . they went down into the earth and then came back up again."[86]

Researcher and author Rupert Sheldrake has written four books on animals, including *Dogs That Know When Their Owners Are Coming Home*. In the book he asks: "Many people who have owned a pet will swear that their dog or cat or other animal has exhibited some kind of behavior they just can't explain. How does a dog know when its owner is returning home at an unexpected time? How do cats know when it is time to go to the vet, even before the cat carrier comes out? How do horses find their way back to the stable over completely unfamiliar terrain? And how can some pets predict that their owners are about to have an epileptic fit?" In our opinion, Sheldrake is a researcher of "rhapsodic intellect" who dares to assert that animals have much to teach us about biology, nature, and consciousness.[87]

Sheldrake's famous 2005 paper "Listen to the Animals: Why did so many animals escape December's tsunami?" highlights the fact that many animals escaped the great Asian tsunami on Boxing Day, 2004. Elephants in Sri Lanka and Sumatra moved to high ground before the giant waves struck; they did they same in Thailand, trumpeting before they did so. "To explore the potential for animal-based warning systems would cost a small fraction of current earthquake and tsunami research," says Sheldrake. "By doing this research we would be sure to learn something, and could probably save many lives."[88]

The great thirteenth-century woman mystic Mechthild of Magdeburg was born into a wealthy German family and had her life-transforming vision at twelve years old when she saw "all things in God and God in all things." Many decades later in her masterpiece, *The Flowing Light of the Godhead*, she wrote that "The truly wise person kneels at the feet of all creatures and is not afraid to endure the mockery of others."[89]

David Abram reminds us in *Becoming Animal* that to be human is to have very limited access to what is. Clearly, other animals have untold universes of wisdom to teach us. We believe that like a host of world-renowned animal researchers and scientists, several named in this book, it is now time to kneel at the feet of myriad creatures to become students of animal consciousness so that our own individual and collective consciousness may be radically transformed. Our deepest heartfelt desire in writing this book is to *liberate* animals and to *learn* from them. At the same time, we know that without the healing of the tortured animal within us and the visceral experience of our sacred relationship with creation, neither is possible. For as James Hillman asserts: "Cosmology has to change if you want to liberate animals from their Western predicament. And the first step in changing cosmology is returning the soul to the world, thereby releasing soul from entrapment in human subjectivism."[90]

Let us end this part of our initiation into vision with a poem from the female, embodied divine human mystic of the sixteenth century, the Rajput princess, Mirabai. When her husband—the crown prince of Mewar—died, she refused to burn herself on his pyre, became a devotee of Krishna, and spent the rest of her life wandering as an ascetic. In one of her greatest works she wrote:

> Within the body are gardens,
> Rare flowers, peacocks, the inner Music;
> Within the body a lake of bliss
> On it the white soul-swans take their joy.
> And in the body, a vast market—
> Go there, trade.
> Sell yourself for a profit you can't spend—
> Mira says, her Lord is beyond praise.
> Allow her to dwell near Your feet.[91]

In some of the legends that have come down to us about her, Mira wandered, often accompanied by a mysterious, dark blue bird, the traditional color of Krishna's skin.

CHAPTER 3

Preparing The Ground of Initiation

*Our alienation from animals and nature kills our hearts, and we
don't even realize how numb we've become until we witness the beauty
of nature and the wonder of life; something as simple as a squirrel
performing acrobatics as she runs across a telephone wire, a bird
alighting on a tree limb and singing a beautiful melody, a bee circling
a flower, or a child reveling at a line of ants crossing a hiking trail.*
— Marc Bekoff, *The Animal Manifesto*[92]

In the last chapter we offered a portion of the vision that is needed in order
for us to surrender to the initiation and transform ourselves enough to live
an embodied, divine life. We need to open to the most amazing possibility,
one that has been hidden in the depths of many mystical traditions, but
now has to be made conscious and pursued with the whole of our being.
This possibility is simply that our destiny is to live in the transfigured
self—a divine self that, like the Divine itself, is utterly transcendent and
utterly immanent and active in lucid, wise compassion on every level. To
arrive at such a vision, which is the essential vision of Jesus, of the prophet
Mohammed, and of the extraordinary evolutionary mystics named above,
three things are necessary.

1) We must unlearn our addiction to transcendence as a way of
escaping the mess and torment of reality. We are not transformed
by spiritually bypassing heartbreak, but rather, by allowing
heartbreak to alchemically transmute the lead of our apathy,

narcissism, entitlement, and arrogance into the gold of naked, shameless, audacious love and compassionate commitment to alleviating the suffering of all living beings.

2) We must abandon our fantasy of the uniqueness of human consciousness. For example, while an octopus is presently incapable of taking an intelligence test designed by and for humans, its awareness is complex and astonishing, and when we humbly contemplate it, we will quite naturally stand in awe.

3) We must unlearn all the religious, social, and cultural messages that have driven us to be dissociated from and repulsed by our physical and animal nature, so that the tremendous love and energy stored in them can permeate our full being.

The clearest and richest, most realistic path that has been opened up to us in many mystical systems, notably the Christian and alchemical and Sufi traditions, has essentially three stages in the journey to the full embodiment of our divinity:

~In the first stage, we need for the sake of our evolution to learn slowly how to separate ourselves from our spiritual, emotional, and physical ego-self so as to open more and more to the Light of the divine Self. This requires intense meditation, prayer, and mystical practice and the view that the greatest mystics have given us of being a hologram of the complete Divine—a drop in an infinite ocean of light, connected to the source of the ocean's power and to every other pulsing drop. This stage ends with an unmistakable experience of the Light as the ground of reality and the presence and force living in and as everything.

~In the second stage, this experience becomes normal and the steady ground of our perception. What we then need to do is to marry what we have discovered of the Light—its freedom, its compassion, its blissful truth and intensity—with all the parts of ourselves we journeyed beyond to reach the Light. This means opening our mental life to being infused and guided by the Light, opening our emotional world with all its hurt, fantasy, shadow, and yearning to the glory of the heart. This means invoking and pulling the Light down into the depths of our bodies.

What we are essentially participating in, in this stage, is the way in which the transcendent Light takes form, lives in form, and when made increasingly conscious, subtly transfigures the whole being. The divine Self is revealed in this stage not only as the infinite expanse of luminous awareness, but also as the life in every wriggling worm, the wild outpouring of song from every bird, the moist, lush, green depths of the forest, and the holy power of the waves pounding the shore.

~In the third stage, the deepening and grounding of this amazing experience opens us to the mystery of being transformed into what the alchemists call the *philosopher's stone*—a being at one with the One, living the embodied mystery of the deepest intercommunion with all of reality, in blissful participation in the interdependence of everything. This stage is known in alchemy as the simple thing, the *res simplex*. While we need to honor this stage and keep it in heart and mind, we also need to be aware of the challenges it will compel us to meet.

It is relatively easy to illumine the mind. It is harder to open the heart and infuse its turbulence with the steady radiance of the soul. The hardest task as all, the evolutionary mystics have found, is to allow the Light to enter our bodies deeply and heal our inherited dualisms and so release ourselves from body hatred and the complex systems of self-loathing and angry projection born from it.

What has become clear to us is that there can be no final healing of our separation from our bodies and no final integration of the love and energy and wisdom hidden in our animal selves without the companionship and guidance of a literal, loving animal. Other physical disciplines such as dance, yoga, and the many wonderful body therapies now available and the deeper blessing of sexuality opened up by the tantric systems, can take us very deeply into the body; they can tremendously expand our sense of the body's vastness and sacredness. But it is in our beloved-beloved relationship with a living animal that we are guided into the richest of all embraces of our animal self.

Imagine if you could be so illumined by grace that you could love your companion animal with the same awed, dazzled, full-hearted, full-bodied way that Kit Smart loved his cat, Jeoffry. Imagine what that love would not only give your companion animal, but what it would awaken in you—nothing less in fact than what Rumi called, "a new kind of love/ neither above nor below," a love of your whole being for another whole being centered in your awakened heart but radiating through all the cells of your body. This is the love indigenous peoples know and have kept vibrant and alive through all the millennia of separation; this is the love that Carolyn's dogs and Andrew's cats have initiated them into. It is from this embodied divine human love, so simple and natural, that increasingly transfigured human beings will co-create with the Divine, a new world.

Andrew and Jade

A year after Andrew met the old Turkish woman at Rumi's tomb, he had an extraordinary confirmation of what she had told him from an old indigenous sage. One of Andrew's most beloved teachers was the great aboriginal elder, Bob Randall. One evening, the two of them were sitting by a crackling fire in the open, moonlit desert near Uluru. Bob had been explaining to him his tribe's vision of what he called *kanyini*, the web of interconnected, reverent, and respectful relationship that Bob called "the truth in action of the unseen great one who can never be named." Bob paused for a long time and then said to Andrew, "You know why you love cats so passionately?"

"You tell me. I can make up something of course. I'm not an Oxford don for nothing."

Bob laughed sardonically. "You're English too. In my experience, the English are never short of words."

Bob turned towards Andrew and looked deep into his eyes.

"You love cats not just because they give you unconditional love. They do, but that is just the beginning of what they give you. The unseen great one has sent you cats to teach you how to love yourself as they love themselves and how to love as they do, with their whole soul, mind, and body centered in an open heart. You have come a long way in your search but your cats will guide you more deeply into love than even your greatest human teachers. It will be they who will guide you into a visceral, natural knowledge of what I call *kanyini,* and that knowledge will change everything for you."

As I lay down that night, stretched out on the sand under the stars in the desert, covered by a simple blanket, I could not sleep. Memories of all the cats I had known and loved since my childhood returned to me.

I remembered sitting in my grandmother's drawing room in her house in south India, her three Siamese cats squatted by me on a white sofa as my grandmother played Chopin nocturnes on her big black piano. Smeared with dust light from the open windows, they sat supernaturally still with their rhinestone-studded leather collars, their pointed ears cupped forward. As the music penetrated me again with its poignant sadness, I realized that from my earliest childhood, the mystery of music and the mystery of cats had always been intertwined in my soul and that my grandmother, who had been a concert pianist in her youth and had lived her wild and troubled life surrounded by the Siamese cats she loved, had given them both to me.

My grandmother was clairvoyant too, with a gift for reading cards and tea leaves; she was a mystic also, aghast sometimes at the apocalyptic visions she repeatedly had. The only person she had confided her gifts and the joy and suffering they brought her was me.

Suddenly as I stared at the dense swirl of stars above me in the Australian bush, I realized that I too, would inherit these gifts, inextricably fused with as I saw clearly now, an abiding wonder at the power of music and the revelatory beauty of cats.

Other memories returned to me as if rearranged in a pattern that confirmed and made vividly personal what the old Turkish woman and Bob Randall had told me. The experience went on all night, but I will present here only four subtle epiphanies.

When I was twenty-five, I traveled throughout Sri Lanka with an old Buddhist woman. We visited a wildlife park, staying in a crumbling Colonial game lodge by the side of a waterhole. On the last afternoon of a four-day visit, we were driving through the park when our driver suddenly jerked our old, green battered jeep to a halt and pointed. There in front of us lying serenely in a sunlit clearing was a sleeping female leopard and four tiny leopard cubs drinking from her exposed belly. The driver whispered, "Send her love." And so, we did for almost an hour in silence. Indescribable peace filled the three of us.

Later my old Buddhist friend wrote to me, "All I can say of that hour is that for the first time in my life, I tasted Nirvana, the peace at the core of reality that I had read about and prayed endlessly for but never known for all my hours of prayer and meditation. I had expected to taste it in the company of my teachers but had never done so. How strange that a leopard and her cubs in a sunlit clearing gave me what I had so long been looking for. As I write this to you, I know I will die soon and that I will die happy."

Lying on the desert sand as I remembered word for word what my old friend had written to me in her spidery writing, the peace that had filled us then filled me again so deeply that I couldn't move.

Then I remembered what happened 18 years later, when I was 43. I was in the backyard of my house in Las Vegas holding in a dark blue velvet shawl the stiff body of my first cat beloved, Purrball. My husband Eric and I had dug a hole in the hard desert ground and were going to bury her with all the roses from our rose garden and letters of gratitude from both of us for all the love she had filled our lives with and a list of the hundred names we had created for her and recited as we went shopping to the supermarket twenty minutes away. I was about to lower her adored body for the last time into the gaping black grave when I heard distinctly a soft female voice say, "Look up." I looked up into the stark pigeon-blue desert sky and there, for one ecstatic second, I saw a vast golden mother cat with wings of light streaming in all directions. I knew with a certainty that I cannot explain or apologize for that Purrball was returning to her original source, the great cat of the sky from whom all cats are unique emanations.

Many years later I was in the Ecuadorian Amazon in a Stone-Age village talking through an interpreter with an 80-year old Actua shaman. I told him of what I had seen on that anguished and astounding afternoon in a vacant Las Vegas suburb. He laughed, leant forward, grabbed my shoulders, shook me and said, "You saw the mother of the great cat from whom all cats come and to whom they all return. I too am a cat and I have seen her many times. It is a blessing. Never forget it. All animals and everything that exists have their own great mother. That is one of the forms of the infinite mother. This we have always known."

As I lay awake, unable to move on the desert sand, the holy wizened smiling face of the Actua shaman appeared above mine briefly. Immediately another memory returned with an intensity so real, everything dissolved around me.

I found myself in South Africa, two years before in Timbavati, the place where I had visited the white lions many times. I was sitting in a jeep in the late morning sun staring at Mandla, king of the white lions, sitting with his back turned in his enclosure 100 yards away. He'd been placed in the enclosure a week before to sequester him after a fight with a tawny lion that had nearly killed him. I myself had nearly died four days before. My gall bladder had exploded and only a six-hour operation in a bush clinic had saved my life. I had come in the jeep to visit Mandla, thinking to commiserate with him.

As my gaze caressed Mandla's back, the king turned, got to his feet, strode majestically right up to the fence that only barely separated him from the jeep I was sitting in. He was now ten feet away from me. He lifted his blazing, serene blue eyes to mine and suddenly with an overwhelming ferocity and with his whole body trembling, Mandla roared at me. My whole being, with all the self-pity and fear my recent brush with death had installed in it, melted away; that unspeakably piercing fierce, noble roar killed and resurrected me at the same time, felled the sentimental coward in me and rebirthed me in the king of the white lion's own courage.

It was as if the ruler of the natural world was saying to me with that roar, "There is no time left in our world hurtling to destruction for anything but lion-hearted courage in action. No time for self-pity, no time to dwell on the wounds of the past, however bloody, or the price you will have to pay again and again for what you must stand up for. You are a warrior for God and nature as I am. Give everything you have and are to the great battle. Nothing less is worthy of me whom you say you love, and nothing less is worthy of you.

Sitting in the jeep, tears of wonder and gratitude streamed down my face. I had been taken to the edge of death, to be made open enough to receive directly from the king of nature the transmission of lion-hearted love in action. Since that day everything I am and write and do has been grounded in that sublime roar.

I lay on the desert sand in Australia drowned in peaceful amazement at what Bob Randall's words had inspired. I tried to tell him when I woke up what had happened. He smiled and stopped me.

"I know it already. I was with you. Keep what you've learned to yourself until it has truly changed you and then only speak of it. When you do, make sure you make it clear that what you were given to experience, amazing as it now seems to you, is what Australian aborigines experience quite naturally and any human being with an open heart and mind can know if they truly want to."

As I sit in my study writing these words in Oak Park in February, 2019, I realize how in the years since that initiation in the bush, grace has helped me integrate what I learned then into my relationship with the cat who is now the center of my life, Jade. She is at once my sweetest friend, my guide into more and more tenderly embodied love, my teacher of peace and restorative rest, my constant seducer into joy and play amidst all the gloom of the darkening world crisis. Being woken up regularly at 4:00 A.M. to feed her salmon Fancy Feast is a tiny price to pay for the wisdom the Garbo of calicos keeps streaming towards me and keeps patiently and mischievously reminding me of when my heart darkens with heartbreak or my mind grows rigid with despair.

Just last week I was lying on my bed on a steel gray winter afternoon in Chicago after a day of horrifying news and fruitless telephone calls, lost in the loneliness that has often afflicted me. Jade leapt onto the bed, crawled onto me, lay down on my heart center, started to purr deeply and stared with her shining black eyes into mine. All grief and self-pity at my isolation vanished as I realized and the words came clearly and fresh minted, "How can you go on telling yourself the story you've been telling yourself nearly all your life? God has sent you your divine beloved who is opening to you the mysteries of embodied, divine love. You thought you would find your beloved in a human being. Well, your beloved happens to be a cat."

I smiled ecstatically at Jade and she blinked and yawned as if to say, "At last you've got it. Now go to sleep with me and wake up refreshed, and go back to whatever it is you do."

Carolyn and Sammy

During the 1990s while living Northern California, I journeyed back and forth many times from there to the Hopi Reservation in Northern Arizona. I had been away from the area for five years, but in the year 2000, I set out on a return journey and arrived on July 20. My first stop was the Hopi Cultural Center which contained a hotel, a restaurant, and a museum.

I remembered that the Cultural Center was notorious for the numbers of hungry "res dogs" that would gather around the restaurant entrance in search of scraps from tourists passing by. As I drove up to the Cultural

Center, I spotted one such creature in the distance lying on the sidewalk in the shade. Something about her riveted me, and I slowly walked up to her as her tail wagged and she looked wistfully into my eyes. I soon noticed that even as every rib in her body was visible, so too was the fact that she was very pregnant. My heart was immediately shattered as I allowed myself to fathom her protruding ribs and bloated belly. I had no dog food with me, but I raced to the restaurant and ordered a few hamburger patties and poured her a bowl of water. I didn't want to feed her too much, too fast, but after slowly providing her the feast, I sat down beside her and began to talk with her.

She was a pit bull with Staffordshire terrier markings—the brindle coat with a white blaze on the chest. Her ears were not cropped as some pit bulls are, but rather, stuck out horizontally from her head making her look a bit like the front end of an airplane. It was a blazing hot day, and I kept pouring water in the bowl so that she would get plenty of relief from the heat. I also noticed that she had a broken foot and many broken teeth.

When I initially met this amazing being, I had no thought of adopting her. No doubt she belonged to someone on the res, but if so, they had done a pathetic job of looking after her. I left the Cultural Center and drove to where I would be staying for five nights, but I was profoundly haunted by my encounter with this strange, lovable dog. The next day, I returned to the Center and found her lying near the same spot. I had purchased some dry dog food, and I approached her again with food and water as her tail wagged even more energetically than the day before. I repeated this ritual at least twice a day for another four days, and each time she saw my truck, her tail began wagging. By this time, I had decided that if she was still at the Center the fifth day, the day I was leaving, I would take her with me. Indeed she was there, and I took her.

I drove to Tucson where I had arranged to stay with friends, but friends who had cats and who were not at all prepared to host both me and a dog. I called a local veterinary hospital in Tucson and asked if I might board her there, but because she had no vaccinations and no medical records, they were reluctant, but told me to bring her in anyway. No sooner had we arrived, than she went into labor and delivered her puppies. Three were dead, but six survived. She was then given vaccinations, medications, and supplements that put her on the mend just in time for our journey home to New Mexico. When we returned home our vet attended to her broken foot and broken teeth—just some of the battle scars she had sustained in her lifetime.

At home I had a wonderful basset hound named Fred, and as I pondered a possible name for my new pit bull friend, I decided on Ethel—Fred and Ethel, the two immortal characters from the 1950s television comedy, "I Love Lucy." My Fred and Ethel became fast friends, and I delighted in both of them until Fred passed in 2005. Going forward, it would be just me and Ethel.

In 2008, at what my vet guessed was the age of 12, Ethel began acting strangely, as if she had developed some sort of cognitive disorder. She was tormented with separation anxiety, and it became challenging to leave her alone when I needed to teach my classes at the local community college. In September, 2009, we moved to Boulder, Colorado, and Ethel's behavior became even more extreme. I took her to the local vet. She was examined and tested positive for Cushing's Disease. Her anxiety and pain increased to the point where she needed to be medicated around the clock, which meant that her life was mostly about sleeping with very little quality left to it.

I set a date with the vet for putting her down and went about trying to prepare myself for the enormous loss I would feel over her death. She had been with me everywhere except at work, and when I worked at home, she was always near me. In the evening, she snuggled with me in our chair, and at night, she slept on my bed.

Johann Sebastian Bach is my favorite composer, and while working at home, his music was often the dominant sound in our house. Frequently, *The Well-Tempered Clavier, Book 1,* graced Ethel and my last days together. As we listened to Bach, the tears rolled down my face uncontrollably, knowing that in just a day or so—then in just a few hours, we must say goodbye.

I told our wonderful vet that I did not want to stand beside a cold exam table when Ethel was put down, but that I wanted to lie down beside her and hold her. She agreed and helped us situate in a special room in her clinic for the heartbreaking occasion. As I lay down on the mattress with Ethel and the first injection was given, the vet asked if I would like some soft music. I told her that I would, and of course, the moment she turned on the CD player, the strains of *The Well-Tempered Clavier, Book 1,* filled the room. The floodgates opened and I didn't stop crying for at least two days. And now, sitting here writing these words, Ethel sweetly stares at me from the photo on a nearby shelf, alongside her ashes and a plaster of Paris paw print created for me by the cremation staff.

What I experienced with the loss of Ethel was far more than heartbreak. Never in my life has grief swallowed and possessed me as it did in the days following her death. I do not exaggerate when I say that she took a part of my soul with her. Ethel was a very old soul who had been through many battles and had acquired many, many scars. It was as if those battles prepared her to meet me, not someone who abused her, but someone whose rough edges didn't allow them to fully appreciate her unconditional love of me until she departed. In those days, I did not know what I know now, nor had I experienced what I have experienced since her death that has softened me and tempered my egoic rigidity.

Over the years I have noticed that many LGBTQ people seem to have a special affinity for animals and seem to "require" them in their lives. How not? Do our beloved furry friends care if we are gay or straight or celibate or transgendered? They do not care if we are hardened criminals or societal pariahs or "the great unwashed." They are simply there for and with us. They see us in ways that we cannot possibly see ourselves.

There are many things about Ethel that I wasn't allowed to know: When was she born and where? How did she end up on the Hopi Reservation? What was her story? How did she get the broken foot and all the broken teeth she came with? Those questions nagged me during our almost ten years together, and they always will. I could have spent money on pet psychics and animal communicators to give me answers, but the bottom line is, I didn't want to know.

Throughout my years as a psychotherapist, when a client was struggling with the loss of a pet, I would suggest that they not get another one until they had given themselves a six-month grieving period for the pet they had just lost. Wonderful suggestion, right? The long and the short of my story is that twelve days after Ethel passed, I adopted Sammy, a Labrador–pit bull mix who looked very much like Ethel. Sammy was two years old when I adopted him, and he was far more energetic than Ethel had ever been. We went to obedience school, and he learned quickly basic commands and behavior. Yet I was not bonded to him as deeply as I was with Ethel. How could I have been?

I struggled with moments of regretting adopting Sammy from time to time, always returning to the day I left the local humane society shelter after six other people wanted him, but for whatever reason, the staff chose me as his new owner. Sammy is larger and leaner than Ethel and not as shamelessly affectionate as she was. Because he wasn't as demonstrative, I felt distance between us, and because he wasn't Ethel, and my broken heart had not healed, I simply resigned myself to the relationship that was and stopped longing for one that wasn't.

But animals and humans find ways to bond deeply that are not planned or obvious and that may even seem impossible. Sammy has been in my life for nine years, and over that time, we have bonded deeply—in a different way than I bonded with Ethel. He did not come into my life from an ugly, abusive past, nor did he carry the battle scars she carried. For that reason, he was not as needy as Ethel and could easily be more independent. Nevertheless, we have bonded deeply, and one of our favorite activities besides playing fetch-ball in the park, is snuggling in a chair or on my bed. In these mutual adoration sessions, we gaze into each other's eyes and cuddle affectionately. For me, it is a form of meditation in which I drink in unconditional love, and Sammy radiates with the joy of being adored and cherished by his special human. Our relationship is now solid and serene, and I give thanks many times each day for his loving, loyal, protective presence in my life. I've stopped longing for another Ethel as my companion and cherish my Sammy, now a senior dog. I now realize that a wisdom surpassing my own intellect designed us for each other's lives.

Shortly after Ethel's death, I discovered "A Dog's Prayer." I know that Sammy would speak such words to me aloud if he could:

A Dog's Prayer

Thank you, my beloved friend, for your kind treatment. No heart in all the world is more grateful for your kindness than the loving heart of me.

Your voice is the world's sweetest music, as you know by the fierce wagging of my tail when your footstep falls upon my waiting ear. I am always near and hope you will never cease talking to me for I will always be listening.

You kept me safe in a cold and bitter world. There is no greater glory than the privilege of sitting at your feet keeping you company.

You kept my pan filled with fresh water though I could not tell you that I was thirsty. You fed me clean food to keep me well to romp and play, to walk by your side and always do your bidding, willing and able to protect you with my life had there ever been a need.

And, my friend, now that I no longer enjoy good health, and we know that I am dying, do not make heroic efforts to keep me going. I am not having any fun. Please see that my trusting life is taken gently. I shall leave this earth knowing with the last breath I draw that my fate was always safest in your hands.

Blessing Our Divine Animal Within

As we undergo this momentous and sometimes grueling blessing of our divine animal, two things should inspire us:

The first source of inspiration should be the growing resistance and brave defiance of animals themselves against the long and brutal history of human cruelty. They are sacrificing themselves to wake us up to the urgent need for the kind of transformation we are proposing in this book.

In 1975 the Australian Peter Singer published his groundbreaking book, *Animal Liberation*. In this book Singer demolished the Cartesian model that treated animals as mere machines and argued that the progressive credo of providing "the greatest good for the greatest number" must now be extended to embrace animals. In that regard, animals should be liberated immediately from their slavery in scientific labs, factory farms, circuses and zoos.

In his great book, *Fear of the Animal Planet*,[93] the historian Jason Hribal takes a revolutionary but logical step beyond Singer. Hribal reverses the usual human perspective and tells the story of liberation from the point of view of animals. For Hribal the issue isn't merely the pain and degradation animals suffer, but consent.

Confined animals haven't given their permission to be held in captivity, compelled to work, fondled, or put on public display to earn their owners millions.

With icy rage, Hribal excavates the hidden history of captive animals as active agents in their own liberation; he takes us behind the scenes of circuses and animal parks, exposing methods of training involving unimaginably sadistic forms of discipline and punishment, where elephants and chimps and other animals are routinely beaten and terrorized into submission. For the first time we are compelled to witness from the animal's perspective the brutal trainers, the heartless dealers in exotic species, conscienceless zookeepers and blood-drunk hunters who slaughter the parents of young elephants and apes in front of their young before they capture them. Hribal takes us inside the cages, tents, and tanks where captive elephants, apes, and sea mammals are imprisoned in wretched conditions with little or no medical care.

Hribal's unique and profoundly inspiring achievement is to show us a history of violent resistance from the animals to such abuses. In his searing book there are stories of escapes, work stoppages, gorings, rampages, bitings, and what can only be called revenge killings. Each trampling of a brutal handler with a bull hook, each mauling of a mocking visitor, each drowning of a sadistic trainer is a crack in the old order that treats animals as property, as engines of profit, as mindless objects of exploitation and abuse.

Hribal's heroic profiles in animal courage show how most of these acts of resistance, violent though they are, were motivated by the animal's abusive treatment and the miserable conditions of their confinement. These animals are far from mindless. Their actions reveal memory, not mere conditioning, contemplation not instinct and, thrillingly, discrimination, not blind anger. Again and again, the animals are demonstrated to target only their abusers, often taking extreme pains to avoid trampling innocent bystanders. In other words, what Hribal shows us is the truth of animals acting in outrage from a moral conscience.

So, in honor of Hribal, let us now praise rebellious animals and let us be brave enough to be worthy of their tragic rebellion.

Contemplate the case of Jumbo the Elephant, at the time, the world's most famous animal. He was captured in East Africa in 1965. Jumbo became the star attraction of P. T. Barnum's circus. While he earned millions for his owners, he was treated horrifically for most of his short life. He was confined to a small compartment with a concrete floor that mangled his feet and made his joints arthritic. He was trained brutally and shackled in leg chains, jabbed with a lance, beaten with ax handles, drugged and fed beer to make him stagger drunkenly. He was shipped back and forth across the country on the Barnum train and forced to perform two shows a day, six days a week. At the age of 24, Jumbo had finally had enough.

On a September night in Ontario, Jumbo and his sidekick, the small elephant called Thom Thumb, broke free from their handlers, wandered away from the tent towards the train tracks. As P. T. Barnum later told the story, Jumbo pushed his friend, Thom Thumb, safely off the tracks and then tried to ram an oncoming train. After his death, an autopsy was performed. In his stomach was found a slew of metallic objects he had been fed over the years: keys, screws, bolts, pennies and nickels—his reward for giving joy to hundreds of thousands of people.

Contemplate Tatiana the Tiger, confined for years in a small enclosure in the San Francisco Zoo. She reached her limit of endurance one Christmas Day after being tormented by three teenage boys. She leapt the 12-foot-high wall, grabbed one of the boys in her paws and eviscerated him. Then she stalked the zoo grounds for the next half hour bypassing many other visitors until she spotted the two other boys and mauled them badly before being gunned down by police.

Contemplate Moe, the chimpanzee. He was an unpaid Hollywood actor who, when he wasn't working, was locked in a tiny cage in West Covina. He made multiple escapes and fiercely resisted his recapture. He bit four people and punched at least one police officer. After his escape he was sent off to miserable confinement at a sordid place called Jungle Exotics. In 2008, Moe escaped one last time into the San Bernardino mountains and has never been heard from since.

Contemplate Buddha, the orangutan [aka Clyde] who co-starred with Clint Eastwood in the movie, *Every Which Way but Loose*. One day on the set, Buddha stopped working, refusing to perform any more of his idiotic routines. In full view of the crew his trainer repeatedly clubbed him on the head with a hard cane. One day towards the end of filming, Buddha filched some donuts from a table on the set. He was seized by his furious keeper, taken back to his cage and beaten to death with an ax handle. Buddha's name was not listed in the film's credits.

Contemplate lastly the story of Tilikum, the orca. At the age of two, Tilikum was seized from the freezing waters of the North Atlantic off the coast of Ireland. He was then shipped to Vancouver Island where he was compelled to perform tricks at an aquatic theme park, Sealand. He was also forced into service as a stud, siring numerous calves for exploitation by his captors. Tilikum shared his small tank with two others, Nootka and Haida. In February, 1991, the whale's woman trainer, slipped and fell into the tank. The orcas took their revenge. The woman was tossed back and forth between them and submerged repeatedly until she drowned. Eight years later a 27-year-old man broke into Sealand, stripped off his clothes and jumped into the tank with Tilikum. Tilikum seized the man, bit him sharply and flung him around. He was found floating dead in the pool the next morning. In 2010 Tilikum was a star at Sea World in Orlando. During an event called Dining with Shamu, Tilikum grabbed his trainer, dragged her into the pool and in front of horror-struck patrons, pinned her to the bottom until she drowned. The orca had delivered his third urgent message. He died in captivity at Sea World in 2017.

When animals give their lives to resist our cruelty, isn't it time we find the courage—those of us whom this cruelty shames and appalls—to stand up for them. Isn't it time to build a global movement to wipe these aquatic gulags forever from the face of the earth?

The second source of inspiration is the amazing current research being done on animal intelligence that is revealing the universe that Kabir and Rumi knew and which the indigenous traditions have always known. It is showing us vistas of as yet unlived but possible transformative relationship. Just as the advances in physics are revealing the universe as an interconnected dance of energy, so scientific research is revealing the creation itself as a field of interconnected, astonishingly varied and complex intelligences, all of which have an inherent, sublime function.

Yet in order to prepare the way for our initiatory descent, we must confront the divine animal *within* that alongside millions of external animals throughout human history have been abused, neglected, and tortured.

We have come to believe that until we redeem our own divine animal, we will resist looking fully at the suffering of animals in the external world and will therefore be less committed to alleviating it.

CHAPTER 4

The Tortured Human Animal

In a world order older and more complete than ours, they move finished
and complete, gifted with extensions of the senses we have lost or never
attained, living by voices we shall never hear. They are not brethren, they
are not underlings; they are other nations, caught with ourselves in the net
of life and time, fellow prisoners of the splendor and travail of the Earth.
— Henry Beston[94]

Oh Divine One, Oh Sacred One, look at our brokenness.
We know that in all creation, only the human family
Has strayed from the Sacred Way.
We know that we are the ones
Who are divided, and
We are the ones who must come back together,
To walk in the Sacred Way,
Oh Divine One, oh Sacred One
Teach us love, compassion, and honor
That we may heal the Earth
And heal each other.
— Adapted from the ancient Ojibway prayer[95]

In this universal prayer that all of us can practice we are turning to the
One in shattered humility. We are recognizing before the One the depth
of our dereliction, the depth of our abandonment of our own deep Selves
and of the Sacred Way. We are accepting without illusion the responsibility

to come back together in our sacred minds, hearts, souls, and bodies in the One and act on every level with the love, compassion, and honor such an extreme situation as ours requires. Experience as you enter the field of this prayer, how sustained and supported you are and feel as you surrender more and more to the all-encompassing mystery of the One. And as you experience the peace and energy that flood you from such support, pledge yourself to risk whatever you must risk and do whatever you must do to restore honor to the adoration of the Divine Animal so that a great healing of our bodies and hearts and souls and the body of the Earth can take place.

At every turn, the human species is engaging in the torture of animals. Whether it be the merciless, egomaniacal "sport" of trophy hunting, the ghastly torture of animals on factory farms and in animal testing and vivisection laboratories, the mechanical pulverizing of newborn chickens who are deemed defective, or the carnage of pit bulls mauling each other in a fighting ring, humans have created an Auschwitz for animals on this planet.

How did this happen? How is it that we can consume a juicy steak without considering how the animal we are savoring was raised? How is it that most meat-eaters give little thought to the hormones and synthetic feeds that the meat industry shoves into the bodies of animals to "fatten" them and make their flesh more cosmetically and gastronomically appealing? How can any sentient human being engage in trophy hunting or worse, "canned" hunting in which an animal is kept in a confined area, such as in a fenced-in area, increasing the likelihood of the hunter obtaining a kill? How can we blithely lather our hair and skin with shampoos and lotions that are "safe" for human consumption because a cat or a rabbit suffered third-degree burns or became blind as a result of brutal laboratory tests by cosmetic manufacturers on their skin or eyes?

The Unbearable Animal Within

We are torturing animals because we have spent millennia torturing the animal in ourselves. Specifically, during the last 200,000 years, we have increasingly and systematically distanced ourselves from our own animal nature and mastered a binary perception of "us" and "them" that has visited incalculable brutality on the more-than-human species as well as our own.

The inescapable result of this torture is that we torture the animal in ourselves and therefore cannot bear the innocence of animals or their shameless naturalness. The torture of the animal in us has driven us to become devourers and murderers of life because in creating systems— religious, philosophical, political, and cultural—that despise, humiliate, and denigrate the body and its holy animal desire, *eros,* we have created for ourselves a concentration camp, and the genocide of the animals is our only consolation in this emotional and spiritual gulag.

As David Abram writes in his extraordinary book, *Becoming Animal:*

> Even among ecologists and environmental activists, there's a tacit sense that we'd better not let our awareness come too close to our creaturely sensations, that we'd best keep our arguments girded with statistics and our thoughts buttressed with abstractions, lest we succumb to an overwhelming grief—a heartache born of our organism's instinctive empathy with the living land and its cascading losses. Lest we be bowled over and broken by our dismay at the relentless devastation of the biosphere.
>
> Thus do we shelter ourselves from the harrowing vulnerability of bodied existence. But by the same gesture we also insulate ourselves from the deepest wellsprings of joy. We cut our lives off from the necessary nourishment of contact and interchange with other shapes of life, from antlered and loop-tailed and amber-eyed beings whose resplendent weirdness loosens our imaginations, from the droning of bees and the gurgling night chorus of the frogs and the morning mist rising like a crowd of ghosts off the weed lot. We seal ourselves off from the erotic warmth of a cello's voice, or from the tilting dance of construction cranes against a downtown sky overbursting with blue. From the errant hummingbird pulsing in our cupped hands as we ferry it back out the door, and the crimson flash as it zooms from our fingers.[96]

Commenting on the frequent appearance of animals in human dreams, James Hillman writes that "The animal as hidden benefactor opens into a series of views in which the animal is interiorized into the human soul in one fashion or another. . . ." He notes the commentary of Christian church father Origen from the third century: 'Understand that you have within yourself herds of cattle, flocks of sheep and . . . goats . . . and that the birds of the air are also within you.' They serve a functional purpose inside us."[97] We can't know ourselves, writes Hillman, unless we see ourselves reflected in them.

The more we became estranged from our own animal origins, the more we began to see ourselves and animals as living beings trapped in and defined by a body made of muscles, bones, tendons, and blood. Our ancient ancestors saw the same thing, but also recognized behind the person or animal in its physical form, a soul or spirit that did not end upon physical death. "In this so-called primitive view, the true or essential animal is a *spiritual entity*, and all its external bodily trappings are just that: *external* and nothing more,"[98] writes Ptolemy Tompkins in *The Divine Life of Animals.*

Shamans and medicine men and women and other spiritual leaders always had animals for teachers because it was believed that only by virtue of an alliance with animals could spiritual practitioners become fully human. Tompkins notes that "By the end of the Paleolithic period, some ten thousand years ago, this easy balance between humans and animals and the rest of nature began to slip."[99] With the invention of agriculture, humans relied less on animals for their survival, and "animals went from kindred souls and fellow traders within the larger economy of spirit to simple possessions: important, but essentially inferior beings that we could use for our material or spiritual benefit, whenever and however we wished. Animals were the first true property. The words *cattle* and *capital* derive from the same root."[100] No longer were animals our spiritual peers, and with the dawn of the Christian era, heaven became a rational place, and humans, who were deemed the only rational beings, were the only ones who would be admitted. As a result, "the original mystery that defined our relationship with animals for eons had been replaced by a cold and unfeeling mastery."[101]

The torture of our own animal being internally and of animals externally in the world can only be healed by a full restoration of the divine animal in us—a full restoration of the holiness and sanctity of every cell of the body, of its passions, and its hunger for intimate communion and its longing for the lavish, natural, primordial warmth of love for every embodied thing. This is the revolution that prepares for the birth of the divine human because the divine human cannot be born without the animal in us being blessed, known, and experienced radically as completely holy and sacred.

It is to this revolution that the animals themselves are guiding us at this moment. They are *willing* to guide us because they are supreme masters of surrender, selflessness, unconditional embodied love, and the marvelous forms of instinctual knowledge that are born from the experience of the fusion of spirit and matter. In this book, we not only face squarely the horror of what we are doing to them, but the reason for that horror—the horror we are doing to ourselves in our hatred and contempt for life—in our sanctification of a brutal separation between spirit and matter that allows us to inflate incessant torture on our bodies and sexualities and skin colors—a torture that has driven us to the edge of suicidal nihilism. Only the resurrection of the divine animal in us can heal this horror.

Unless we can accept and bless our own animal nature, we will continue to torture animals and through our brutality, bring about our own demise. Unless we turn to the animals to teach us the secrets they are masters of—embodied love and embodied divine intelligence, we too will die out.

However, there are two terrors that we must overcome with animals:

The first terror is of their embodied innocence—that radiance of presence that lives so effortlessly in them and that we have so desperately lost in our arrogant and futile complexity. We torture them with contempt for their innocence because we are so tortured by the loss of our own. It is to escape the lash of these truths that we torture the natural world.

The second terror that we have of animals is terror of their violence and ferocity. Because we cannot discover the instinctual, pure intelligence that drives the animal's anger and violence, we have fallen prey to a far more corrupt, cold, methodical, dissociated violence that has to destroy the animals so as not to see its ugly and distorted face in the mirror of their instinctual splendor.

Of course, we must not project innocence and benevolence on all animals; we must at once recognize and respect their capacity for violence while acknowledging that sadism and violence for its own sake is rare. We must also responsibly notice any desire within ourselves to conquer, tame or demonize their violence through projected comparison with our own. Indeed, we must not project innocence and benevolence on all animals. We must respect their capacity for violence, and at the same time, we must notice any desire within ourselves of "conquer" or "tame" it.

Human Serial Killers

The connection between animal abuse and neglect and aggression toward other humans is beyond dispute. Michigan State University's Animal Legal and Historical Center reported that:

> There is a significant correlation between acts of cruelty to animals as a child and serious, recurrent aggression towards people as an adult. In fact, one of the most reliable predictors of future violence as an adult is having committed animal abuse as a child. Research in psychology and criminology indicates that people who commit acts of cruelty to animals often do not stop there—many of them later turn on humans. Psychology, sociology, and criminology studies have shown that many violent offenders had committed repeated acts of serious animal cruelty during childhood and adolescence. People who abused pets as children are more likely to commit murder or other violent crimes as adults. In fact, violent criminals are five times more likely to commit violent crimes against people if they did so against animals as youths. There is a further correlation: the most aggressive criminals had committed the most severe acts of animal cruelty in childhood.

> Acts of animal cruelty are not merely signs of a minor personality flaw, but are rather symptomatic of a deep

mental disturbance. Cruelty to animals has been recognized as an indicator of a dangerous psychopathy that claims both animal and human victims. A survey of psychiatric patients who had repeatedly tortured animals found that all of them were also highly aggressive towards people.

Acts of violence beget acts of increased violence. It is a matter of escalation: people who want to victimize start with something they can easily control, then they work their way up. A person who only feels powerful and in control while inflicting pain or death must continually sustain that "high" by committing acts that are more heinous or morbid. The violent act itself must be viewed as dangerous, without regard as to whether the victim is a person or an animal. An example of this escalation is the "Vampire cult leader," Rod Ferrell, who is serving a life sentence for bludgeoning a Florida couple to death. Ferrell first drew the attention of law enforcement in Kentucky, where he was charged with breaking into an animal shelter where two puppies were tortured, killed and mutilated.

The link between animal abuse and violence towards people is supported by studies, which have shown that:

- 100% of sexual homicide offenders examined had a history of cruelty towards animals.
- 70% of all animal abusers have committed at least one other criminal offense and almost 40% have committed violent crimes against people.
- 63.3% of men who had committed crimes of aggression admitted to cruelty to animals.
- 48% of rapists and 30% of child molesters reported committing animal abuse during childhood or adolescence.
- 36% of assaultive women reported cruelty to animals while 0% of non-assaultive women did.

- 25% of violent, incarcerated men reported higher rates of "substantial cruelty to animals" in childhood than a comparison group of non-incarcerated men (0%).
- Men who abused animals were five times more likely to have been arrested for violence towards humans, four times more likely to have committed property crimes, and three times more likely to have records for drug and disorderly conduct offenses.[102]

While vast numbers of humans are compassionately outraged over the torture of animals by our species and are consciously working to alleviate their suffering, many more are oblivious to it as a result of the centuries of objectification and carnage based on the myth of human superiority. We are not exaggerating when we speak of human serial killers because we believe there are five aspects of the serial killer's mind which the majority of our species shares:

1. The serial killer's trauma is expressed as torture. As noted above, the human him/herself is tortured, and their own impotence in the face of suffering expresses itself in torturing other beings who are innocent, weak, and helpless.
2. The serial killer is dissociated from any spiritual Source, leading to a despairing realism that expresses itself in savagery toward life.
3. The serial killer is steeped in absolute narcissism, founded in a secret terror that they have to continue killing in order to keep believing in their own self-empowerment. In fact, this reality is a radical X-ray of humanity in this moment of the collapse of ecosystems and industrial growth civilization. On some level, every human knows the severity of our planetary predicament, but nearly all are unwilling to face that predicament. Lashing out at animals is humanity's feeble attempt at shoring up a rapidly disintegrating self.
4. The serial killer totally lacks empathy which is born from living in a meaningless and merciless world. To be empathic is to be willing to feel one's feelings, and with emotions such as grief, compassion, or caring, questions of meaning become urgent. How much easier

it is to embrace an existence numbed by the soporific of an egoic sense of power and conquest.

5. The serial killer despises innocence because they are inwardly convulsed by horror at the loss of their own innocence. Thus the need to crucify innocence as a way of avoiding the mirror that reveals their own dereliction.

While each of these five are aspects of the serial killer's psyche, they are also aspects of the way industrial growth culture perpetuates a sociopathic worldwide genocide of all living beings. A host of examples abound, one of the most glaring being the documentary, *The Corporation*. Arguably, the modern corporation functions very much like the serial killer, as Noam Chomsky notes: "Corporations were given the rights of immortal persons. But then special kinds of persons, persons who had no moral conscience. These are a special kind of persons, which are designed by law, to be concerned only for their stockholders. And not, say, what are sometimes called their stakeholders, like the community or the work force or whatever."[103]

The genocide of animals reflects not only a collapse of systems and the paradigm of industrial civilization itself, but a collapse of the human psyche and the eruption in it of the darkest and most evil forces in the unconscious. This appalling situation is tragically reinforced by a completely heartless consumerism and a dark passion to dominate nature—a soulless capitalism that is prepared to destroy everything in the pursuit of greed and power, enabled by patriarchal religions.

At the root of all patriarchal religions is the belief in separation, the belief in an off-planet god, a transcendent god that demeans and degrades the creation and who makes life on Earth either an illusion or a valley of sorrows to be endured for another worldly reward. Thus the ecstatic experience of union with reality that reveals the light present in everything that is, is closed off. This appalling tragedy has corrupted human consciousness with a profound, unacknowledged blindness to the beauty and glory of creation and a deep, secret hatred of life. We must face the fact that patriarchal religions reinforce these horrific tendencies through their anthropocentrism, their lack of awareness of the sacredness of all creation, their inherent false privileging of human consciousness above all others, and the dreadful and demeaning messages about animal instinct. For example, Buddhism and Hinduism celebrate the uniqueness of human consciousness as a gateway to liberation in a way that blinds their followers to the presence of alternative and equally powerful and gifted forms of consciousness that exist in animals. Christianity, of course, touts the dominion of humans over all of nature—plant, mineral, and animal.

Derrick Jensen notes in *The Myth of Human Supremacy* that the assumption of human domination "not only eases or erases the consciences of the perpetrators [of cruelty and neglect], but makes resistance to these perpetrators seem futile. . . . It is extraordinarily useful for those whose lifestyles are based on the systematic exploitation of others to pretend that this exploitation is natural. Thus, they needn't worry their consciences about this exploitation, which they no longer perceive as exploitation, and no longer perceive even as 'just the way things are,' but rather as completely expected. Inevitable. Natural."[104]

We believe that a fundamental aspect of our spiritual evolution is a cultivated deepening of our humanity. The question is not, are we good Christians, good Buddhists, good devotees of a particular spiritual teacher, but are we good human beings? As noted above by Ptolemy Tompkins, "only by virtue of an alliance with animals could spiritual practitioners become fully human."[105]

We would like to offer you, dear reader, a direct way of participating in the visceral and amazing work it requires to reconnect with your own animal body, learn truly how to listen to it, and honor in every way its vision and power and capacity for love. This work is extremely demanding because it asks all of us to face the way in which our addiction to mental consciousness has made us torture our own animal bodies and so deepen the traumas that drew us to dissociate in the first place. We will guide you in an unfolding of consciousness to embrace the divine animal within and without in the creation and help you find the energy to rise in honor to protect the creation.

Thus, we offer this prayer:

> *Oh Divine One, Oh Sacred One,*
> *Give us the courage to dare to look*
> *Into the abyss of animal suffering*

In us and around us and caused by us.
Do not let us look away from what we see
In that abyss about ourselves
The cruelty that is born in us
When we are dead to ourselves.
Do not let us despair but fill us
With your love so we
Can continue to try to be worthy
Of the love you never stop showering us with.

The Descent

A Practice to Prepare for the Descent

Communing with the Divine Mother

First practice: Sit comfortably in a chair with eyes closed. Envision the Divine Mother in a form that feels the most tender and nurturing to you. Imagine that she is located within the right side of your chest, and when you have that sense of her presence, bow your head in the direction of your heart. Begin silently thinking the sound *Ma, Ma, Ma* and continue gently. Just gently continue saying it with tremendous devotion. Focus on all of creation and the overwhelming love with which she created it. Pour your own love into this, and feel her unconditionally loving and supporting you, no matter what you believe or don't believe. Do all of this very gently for about ten minutes.

Second practice: Lie down on the floor, get comfortable with eyes closed, and imagine a large, black magnet beneath you in the shape of your body. Imagine that all of the suffering you are going through both present and past is being extracted by that pulsing black magnet. As you do that, keep the *Ma* sound in your heart. Allow it to extract the illusion of right and wrong as well. And then imagine above you in the shape of your body, the body of the Mother. It is pouring golden light into your body as the dark mystery of her takes all of the pain out of your body. Let go and surrender into it. Again, feel the unconditional love that the golden light pours into you. Do this for approximately ten minutes.

Third practice: Sit back up in your chair, settle in with eyes closed, and imagine her standing above you in whatever form you want her to be in. (She may be standing beside you but over you as you are sitting.)

She is cupping her hands in golden light and she's pouring that light into the center of the top of your skull, your crown chakra. Allow that golden light to radiate in your crown and down into the area of your third eye, which becomes like a diamond. Allow the golden light to descend into your face and neck and into the throat chakra, becoming a bright red rose. Then allow it to descend into your chest and surround your heart. Feel your heart as a radiant sun of love and compassion and passion. Then the light descends into your solar plexus/third chakra which is your power center—the center of the will. Feel the power there, and then remember that your power is in your surrender and feel the golden light in your solar plexus as power *through* surrender. Then allow the golden light to descend into your belly and genitals, the second chakra. Allow all sexual pain to be illumined and cleaned out. Then allow the light to go to the first chakra of survival and life force energy. Then allow it to descend into your legs and feet, releasing you from karmic bonds. Then rest in that bodily glow. As with the former two practices, do this for about ten minutes.

CHAPTER 5

When We Cannot Look, We Cannot Act

*Animals are destitute of reason . . . and . . . it is
nature that acts in them mechanically.*
— René Descartes, "Discourse on Method," Part 5

*The greatness of a nation and its moral progress can
be judged by the way its animals are treated.*
— Attributed to Mahatma Gandhi

Now we must enter the second stage of the initiation: The descent. The descent into as complete a facing as we can bear of the horror, ignorance, and heartlessness we are inflicting on our relations, the animals. It has been Carolyn and Andrew's experience that it is impossible either to face squarely or to bear what we have to bear without a practice that can give us a taste of the transfigured being that we are being birthed into through this global dark night. We have found from long and profound attempts of our own that it is only when we ground our whole being—heart, mind, soul, and body—in the all-transfiguring Light of the Mother that we find the courage to gaze into the boiling abyss of the human destructiveness we all collude with. It is only through the grace of this all-transfiguring light that we can create a container strong and spacious and radiant enough to hold the savage agony of heartbreak that must inevitably follow on any clear recognition of what we have done and continue to do.

Thus we offer you these practices with the hope that they will give you the courage, illumination, and inner peace that they have given us.

107

Inspired by the vision we have offered, we are now ready to face without illusion or the need to dissociate, the appalling facts of what is happening to animals on Earth. This stage is a stage of descent into the human shadow and its devastating effect on the creation. The meaning of descent is twofold: One the one hand, it will give us a stark and inescapable permanent knowledge of everything in us that needs urgently to be transformed. On the other, it will open us to new energies of connection, joy, and hope that will fuel our determination to protect the creation.

What we've discovered on our own journeys is that you can only go as deep into the darkness of the shadow as you have been fortified and inspired by divine vision. If you are not grounded in the vibrant possibilities that Section One has revealed to you, you will find yourself wanting to distract yourself from the horror and agony we need to face. If you have allowed the vision we have presented to infuse you with passion and determination, you will be able to meet the worst and most potentially paralyzing facts with equilibrium, compassion, and a profound desire to transform the consciousness and actions that keep worldwide genocide of animal species going. No one would want to face what we are asking you to face without first being filled with the extraordinary possibilities that a vision of unity with the creation opens up to us. So as you descend with us remember to keep practicing presence and ground yourself in its spacious peace.

The Sobering Data

The human shadow consists of those parts of ourselves that we send away into unconsciousness because they are too painful or too damaging to our ego identity to contemplate. However, they do not vanish, but rather remain in the unconscious and continue sometimes even more strongly for being ignored. We then project those aspects of the shadow onto other living beings or because of our shadow material, we may be compelled to ignore the suffering of other beings, perhaps even "taking pride" in our awareness of their suffering, which cannot be awareness at all if our own responsibility for it is not acknowledged. This is especially true, as you'll discover, of the way we treat animals or allow them to be treated.

In presenting the sobering data of our treatment of animals,[106] we do not wish to overwhelm you with grim statistics of animal abuse, neglect, and torture. It is not our desire to beat you over the head, but we also understand that when we are unable to look at the severity of the genocide of the more-than-human world, the revolution in perception which is crucial in order to reverse the genocide becomes impossible. Only a confrontation with the full extent of what is happening to animals can awaken our conscience and compel us to discern what urgent action must be taken not only on behalf of animals but also to preserve human dignity and the integrity of the human soul.

Here we present the data as cleanly and un-hysterically as possible because we are aware from our own experience how devastating and paralyzing such a presentation can be. Nevertheless, we are asking you to read the data slowly and to allow the full atrocity of what it presents to sink deeply and irrevocably into the heart. We could suggest that you pause after each section for five minutes of contemplation, so that you can find the inner stability to be able to continue to bear what must be borne. If we are ever to take action on behalf of the non-human world—and ourselves—we must know that indeed, its fate is invariably our own.

Instead of allowing this data to paralyze us, let us have the courage to allow it to humble us finally so as to make us open to the mystery of the creation that is waiting to guide us forward. We cannot go into this mystery except on our knees, aghast at the horror we have allowed to expand everywhere, humbled by our responsibility for its savagery, heartbroken at the hubris of our cruelty and seared open to the need for mercy, grace, and totally unfamiliar new knowledge. This is our last and best hope.

When we speak of an Auschwitz for animals, we mean that:

- 56 billion land animals are killed for food each year.[106]
- Researchers note that not only are standard slaughter practices unethical, there are often reports of intentional abuse of animals by workers. For example, at the Pilgrim's Pride slaughterhouse, which supplies KFC restaurants, a videotape shows workers kicking and stomping on chickens and smashing them against

walls. Employees also ripped birds' beaks off, twisted their heads off, and broke them in half—while the birds were still alive.[107]

- Hogs, unlike cattle, are dunked in tanks of hot water after they have been stunned to soften their hides for skinning. Stunning is not always successful, and secret videotape from an Iowa pork plant shows hogs squealing and kicking as they are being lowered into the water.[108]

- Egg-laying hens are debeaked with hot knives to prevent cannibalism and fighting. A typical cage is about 12x20 inches, or the size of a single sheet of newspaper, and contains 4–8 birds. The cages, called battery cages, are stacked floor to ceiling in massive sheds. Hens living on the bottom tiers are showered with excrement. Battery cages are outlawed in some European countries but are still legal in the U.S.[109]

- Castration, dehorning, branding, ear notching, tail clipping, and beak trimming are widely conducted in the U.S. without the use of anesthetics or pain medication. In Canada, local anesthetic is recommended. It is required by law in most cases in the U.K.[110]

- Factory-farmed hogs not only suffer from excessive crowding, stress, and boredom, but also experience breathing disorders because of high concentrations of ammonia from their waste materials. Hogs also experience feet and leg deformities from standing on floors made of improper materials.[111]

- Fur farmers are mainly concerned with preserving the animal's whole coat and often choose the cheapest way to kill animals. Many ranchers use electrocution, which fries the animal inside out, similar to being cooked in a microwave. Some farmers also inject insecticides into the chests of minks. It takes several minutes for the minks to die a painful death.[112]

- Approximately 5,000 Thoroughbred racehorses died between 2003 and 2008. Most of the horses were euthanized after suffering serious injuries on the racetrack. Countless other deaths went unreported because of lax record keeping.[113]

- In Spain, during the festive "Toro Jubilo," gobs of pitch are placed on a bull's horn and then lit on fire. The bull is let loose in the streets, where it runs frantically in pain as the fire burns the bull's horns, eyes, and body while the spectators cheer. The bull can be on fire for hours.[114]

- Trophy Hunting: Trophies of more than 1,200 different kinds of animals were imported during the decade studied, including nearly 32,500 trophies of the Africa Big Five species: Approximately 5,600 African lions, 4,600 African elephants, 4,500 African leopards, 330 southern white rhinos, and 17,200 African buffalo. The top ten species imported during the decade were snow geese, mallards, Canada geese, American black bears, impalas, common wildebeests, greater kudus, gemsboks, springboks and bonteboks.[115]

- Canned Hunting: Captive hunting operations—also referred to as "shooting preserves," "canned hunts," or "game ranches"— are private trophy hunting facilities that offer their customers the opportunity to kill exotic and native animals trapped within enclosures. Some facilities have even allowed their clients to kill animals remotely via the Internet. Over 1,000 canned hunting facilities exist in the United States, and canned hunting is a thriving industry in Africa, especially the hunting of lions.

- Trophy hunting originated with imperialists. Empire and trophy hunting have always traveled together because the secret guilt that convulses the empire expresses itself in ever greater enlargements of killing. The current imperial class has perfected the ultimate decadence of canned hunting where all pretensions of heroic hunting have been drowned by creating venues where the "hunter" just walks up and shoots the animal. Thus, canned hunting has made it as easy to kill as ordering a hamburger in a restaurant.

- Vivisection and animal testing: Estimates for the total number of animals used in research worldwide hover between 115 million and 127 million, while estimates for the U.S. specifically hover around 25 million. In the U.S., researchers are not required to report the numbers of rats, mice, and birds used in experiments, and these species combined make up an estimated 95% of all animals used in research.[116]

Laboratory animals are often isolated. On top of the deprivation, there are the experiments. U.S. law allows animals to be burned, shocked, poisoned, isolated, starved, drowned, addicted to drugs, and brain-damaged. No experiment, no matter how painful or trivial, is prohibited—and pain-killers are not required. Even when alternatives to the use of animals are available, the law does not require that they be used—and often they are not.

Animals are infected with diseases that they would never normally contract: tiny mice grow tumors as large as their own bodies, kittens are purposely blinded, rats are made to suffer seizures, and primates' skulls are cut open and electrodes are implanted in them. Experimenters force-feed chemicals to animals, conduct repeated surgeries on them, implant wires in their brains, crush their spines, and much more.[117]

Humans are outraged by the horrific experiments performed on humans in Nazi death camps by Joseph Mengele, but why are we not outraged by what humans are doing to animals through vivisection and laboratory testing?

- Between 1970 and 2010 populations of mammals, birds, reptiles, amphibians, and fish around the globe dropped 52%, says the 2014 Living Planet Report released by World Wildlife Fund (WWF). This biodiversity loss occurs disproportionately in low-income countries—and correlates with the increasing resource use of high-income countries.[118]

- Three-quarters of flying insects in nature reserves across Germany have vanished in 25 years, with serious implications for all life on Earth, scientists say. Insects are an integral part of life on Earth as both pollinators and prey for other wildlife. It was known that some species such as butterflies were declining, but the newly revealed scale of the losses to all insects has prompted warnings that the world is "on course for ecological Armageddon," with profound impacts on human society.[119]

We have kept our sobering data to a minimum because we know from personal experience how devastating and paralyzing contemplating it can be and how easy it is to dissociate from its anguish. But we cannot stress enough how dangerous such dissociation is, not only for the animals but for ourselves. Thus, we offer here two stories from Matthew Scully's

Dominion: The Power of Man, the Suffering of Animals, and The Call to Mercy.

We urge you to read these stories slowly, watching inwardly how we all want to turn away from what is expressed in them—the terrible state of our corrupted and depraved human nature. And yet, without acknowledging that we too participate in this corruption and depravity, we will never find the courage to transmute them.

One of the most sobering aspects of the horror we inflict on animals is the astoundingly lucrative business of killing and smuggling them. Genocide, it seems, is big business, and until we face and end this system of cold evil, all our protestations on behalf of animal rights may cheer us up, but will do nothing to halt the agony.

In a shocking, heartbreaking exposé[120], entitled, "Animal Underworld: Inside America's Black Market for Rare & Exotic Species," Alan Green examines the fate of unwanted animals cast off by U.S. zoos and theme parks. Many of the nation's leading zoos, he reports, sell their unwanted animals—whether surplus, aging and decrepit, or babies bred for sale—to supposedly reputable dealers who, in turn, dump the animals onto roadside attractions, unaccredited petting zoos, private hunting parks, and bogus sanctuaries that will hand over endangered species to anyone for a buck. Using easily doctored documents, the animals are laundered into obscurity, shunted from opportunistic breeders to wretched menageries, auctioneers, backyard hobbyists, and even university research centers. Many of these animals, according to Green, suffer cruel abuse, mistreatment or fatal neglect; some end up as exotic meat on the grocery shelf. He also argues that zoos ignore their own edict by permitting animals to migrate almost uncontrollably into the hands of unaccredited institutions. Working with the Center for Public Integrity, a Washington, D.C.-based nonprofit organization, Green crisscrossed the country, combing thousands of health certificates and interviewing hundreds of people. He tracked smugglers and poachers who traffic in rare species disappearing from their native habitats, which are then sold to "exotic pet" owners. He takes aim particularly at the thousands of Americans who keep dangerous pets like tigers or cougars, inviting human tragedies. A major feat of investigative reporting, this book spells out sensible strategies to clean up this unholy mess, including a proposal that zoos should provide cradle-to-grave care to their denizens. Green's important, eye-opening report could spark a national debate.

In an age in which we are experiencing the rapid and terrifying collapse of all of our illusions and systems, the horror that we are repressing in denial, pointless consumerism, and meaningless hedonism is bound to be expressed in cruelty towards those who are the most vulnerable and innocent.

Animal rights is not just about our being benevolent to animals, but ultimately about saving our own souls and stopping the meaningless nihilism that is corrupting everything we do and creating an unstoppable terminal disaster that will annihilate all life.

In a sense, even "animal rights" is a dualistic term that reinforces the separation that has led to the disaster in the first place. There is no separating the survival of animals from our own survival. Animal rights are an inherent part of human rights.

As we torture animals, so we torture ourselves and each other. In karmic terms, we are building for ourselves a tsunami of negative karma for our own species. We've ignored the reality that the Divine Mother has other children besides us, and as a result of our disregard for Her on myriad levels, we may fulfill the Hopi prophecy that warns us that unless we pay attention to the Mother, She will shake us off like a dog shakes off fleas.

What this book is calling for is nothing less than a revolution in perception that faces squarely our responsibility for the terminal situation we are creating, the bankruptcy of all the religious systems and philosophies that have guided us, the facts of our worldwide genocidal cruelty against the animals and creation in general, and the necessity for a massive spiritual transformation that reveals the equality of all being and the sacredness of every flea, stone, insect, and blade of grass.

In the Upanishads, the great Hindu scriptures, it is written: *The wise see the divine flaming in all creation.* We have no more time left to remain unwise.

The Marriage

the wisdom of the Light and the wisdom of the dark—
the marriage of the serpent and the dove

Now we arrive at the third stage of our initiation. In this stage, we surrender to divine grace and allow its merciful power to marry within us at ever-increasing depths the wisdom of the serpent and the innocence of the dove, the ecstatic wisdom that vision has given us and the tragic, searing wisdom that descent has opened up for us. In our experience the most powerful possible practice that allows grace to work most richly in us is the practice of the prayer of St. Francis, the sublime prayer that many seekers on all paths now use to dedicate themselves to the service of all beings.

A Practice to Prepare You for the Sacred Marriage
Embodying the Prayer for Animals by St. Francis of Assisi

Francis of Assisi lived in twelfth-century Italy and was enamored with nature and animals. He is said to have written a mystical prayer for animals which to this day is used to bless and care for animals throughout the world. We offer his prayer:

> Lord, make me an instrument of your peace:
> where there is hatred, let me sow love;
> where there is injury, pardon;
> where there is doubt, faith;
> where there is despair, hope;
> where there is darkness, light;
> where there is sadness, joy.

O divine Master, grant that I may not so much seek
to be consoled as to console,
to be understood as to understand,
to be loved as to love.

For it is in giving that we receive,
it is in pardoning that we are pardoned,
and it is in dying that we are born to eternal life.
Amen.

We invite you into a practice using this prayer. Begin my sitting calmly in your place of meditation and then begin breathing in and out deeply to steady your mind. You may want to prepare by burning incense and then as you breathe, to place your hand on your heart. When you feel ready, read the entire prayer slowly once through, savoring each word and trying to enter as deeply as you can, the inmost meaning of each phrase. When you have done so, rest for a bit in the sacred emotion the reading will arouse.

I find it helpful at this moment to pray that I might be opened even more deeply to the holy passion of the prayer. It may be helpful to say something like, "May the love speaking this prayer open me completely to itself." Or, "Remove all fear from my mind and heart so that it can go fearlessly into the fire of absolute love."

Then slowly, start to say inwardly for the first time, "Lord, make me an instrument of your peace." Dwell richly on each phrase. For example, what is an "instrument of peace" and what has to be given up to become one? Why does St. Francis seem to stress the holiness of peace above all other aspects of the spiritual life? What is "thy peace"? To each inner question, try to bring the totality of everything that you have understood about these questions from your own experience and the experience of others.

Your mind may begin to wander, perhaps almost immediately. Something about the power and beauty of the prayer scares the mind profoundly. Perhaps it terrifies the ego. Be compassionate with the mind as it tries to evade the seriousness of the prayer's intention, but also try not to let the mind wander too far. As soon as you catch it wandering, bring it back to the line of the prayer it was contemplating before it started to wander.

Slowly, and with as much concentration as you can muster, go through the prayer phrase by phrase, trying to bring everything you know and long for to your inner reading of it. Then, after a brief pause, return to the beginning. Give yourself at least a half hour with this prayer. To enter the silence is the true goal of all prayer. Allow the silence, and stop speaking the words. Rest for a moment or two in the silence. Then recite the prayer once more, dedicating whatever emotions or insights this practice has given you, to the awakening of all sentient beings.

CHAPTER 6

What Is Being Done for Animals

I think I could turn and live with animals,
they are so placid and self-contain'd,
I stand and look at them long and long.

They do not sweat and whine about their condition,
They do not lie awake in the dark and weep for their sins,
They do not make me sick discussing their duty to God,
Not one is dissatisfied, not one is demented with the mania of owning things,
Not one kneels to another, nor to his kind that lived thousands of years ago,
Not one is respectable or unhappy over the whole earth.

So they show their relations to me and I accept them,
They bring me tokens of myself, they evince them plainly in their possession.
— Walt Whitman, "Song of Myself"

The White Lion message, nature's message, is unfolding at this
very moment. It is radiant and magnificent. And it is not
too late. The reality is that potentially, we all have the power
of light—the White Lion within us. The very first step is to
overcome our fears. Thereafter, our hearts will lead the way.
— Linda Tucker, *The Mystery of the White Lions*

In the fields of animal and environmental protection there are
literally thousands of people around the globe who are devoting

their lives—sometimes risking their lives—to help animals and our
environment. Their efforts cover all aspects of stewardship: tireless lobbying
for new anti-cruelty or environmental and species conservation laws or
regulations; organizing or taking part in demonstrations; speaking out
and establishing interest groups; and starting rescue centers for species
as diverse as domestic poultry, on the one hand, and abused elephants,
on the other. Rescue and rehabilitation centers are growing in number
all the time as people are moved to try to take action themselves to
alleviate suffering. Organizations established to enforce animal and
environmental protection laws exist in almost all parts of the world.
— Jane Goodall and Marc Bekoff, *The Ten Trusts: What*
We Must Do to Care for the Animals We Love[121]

Before we celebrate with you and for you some of the truly amazing people who are giving their lives to respond to the genocide of the animals, we want to offer you a practice that you can utilize to work for the liberation of the animals at all moments.

All the people we are celebrating know that all of us are capable of doing what they do if we love enough. They are not interested in being icons; they are incendiaries of love, and they are burning not to be admired but to help us break into flames.

This practice is about breaking into flames—flames of passionate compassion for the terrible torment that animals are suffering and the terrible torment inflicted by those who inflict such suffering on themselves.

A Practice for Healing Heartbreak for the Animals

Here is a practice to heal your own paralyzed grief at the horror of what's being done to animals. Imagine yourself looking at yourself in the mirror. The person looking in the mirror is your inner Buddha or Christ—the witness in you that knows you are divine. The person you are looking at in the mirror is the biographical, brutalized, traumatized human being, terrified at the beginning to feel something of the unspeakable agony and abomination of animal suffering.

Imagine that all that suffering starts to leave the belly of the person in the mirror in a ball of black smoke. In your divine being, take that black smoke into your infinite heart that you imagine like a stainless blue sky and dissolve it there and keep radiating back to the wreck in the mirror, passionate compassion. Slowly, you will find your heartbroken, human self, revived in joy and power and commitment to stand by and for the animals.

Jane Goodall

In *Hope for Animals and Their World*, Jane Goodall writes that one of the challenges she faced during the writing of that book was just how many admirable efforts are being made to save endangered species all over the world. In this chapter, we want to highlight several individuals whom we consider heroes and heroines of Sacred Animal Activism. We will begin with some far away from the United States and end with more local efforts.

We bow to the beloved Jane Goodall who has spent most of her adult life deeply engaged with animals and who to this day as an octogenarian remains steadfast in her efforts to care for many species beyond the chimpanzees with whom she bonded so deeply in Gombe. In *Hope for Animals and Their World*, Jane highlights several women and men whose herculean efforts are making a difference for a number of species.

Saving the Iberian Lynx

Miguel Angel Simon in the Iberian Peninsula of Spain works closely with Astrid Vargas to save the Iberian Lynx which in 2001 was very near total extinction. Jane visited Simon and Vargas in 2006 to more closely explore their work, which included a captive breeding program to mitigate extinction. In 2008 she learned that by that year, the captive breeding program was ahead of projections. Fifty-two lynx were in captivity, and twenty-four were born in the facility. Jane writes,

> I then heard from Miguel that the number of territorial breeding females was up to nineteen, and there were between seventeen and twenty-one new cubs alive in September,

2008. While the verdict is still out as to whether or not Spain's magnificent Iberian lynx will once again have a suitable habitat that allows it to thrive in the wild—a protected area that is safe from pilgrims, golf courses, and the like—for now, the new is encouraging.[122]

Jane's Additional Captive Breeding Success Stories

In the Gobi Deserts of Mongolia and China, former British Foreign Service officer John Hare has worked for decades to save the Bactrian camel. Without his efforts, the species would already be extinct. Their enemies are humans who hunt them or who prospect for oil in the desert sands, and where nuclear tests are conducted alongside the poisoning of their grazing lands as humans search for gold. They were more endangered than the giant panda.

In 1997 John set up the Wild Camel Protection Foundation to raise funds for conservation efforts to protect the Bactrian camel. John and his foundation started a wild breeding program, and at the end of the first three years of operation, seven wild Bactrian camels were born to eleven wild females and a wild bull camel that had been caught by Mongolian herdsmen.

An exciting success story is the giant panda, mentioned above. By the year 2000, births began to outnumber deaths, and from 2005, there were significant increases in the captive population. This was a result of a changing attitude in managing pandas, the improvement of captive conditions, and an increase in natural settings. As a result, in 2008, there was a 95 percent survival rate in infants compared to a 50 percent survival rate twenty years prior.

In *Hope for Animals and Their World*, Jane relates the successes of efforts to save the Pygmy Hog of India, the Northern Bald Ibis in Europe, the Columbia Basin Pygmy Rabbit in America, the American Prairie Chicken, the Asian Vultures of India, Nepal, and Pakistan, and the Hawaiian Goose or nene.

Jane may be contacted at: http://www.janegoodall.org/

Frans de Waal: Researching Animal Intelligence

Frans de Waal's research into the innate capacity for empathy among primates has led him to conclude that non-human great apes and humans are simply different types of apes, and that empathic and cooperative tendencies are continuous between these species.

De Waal penned a beautiful *Wall Street Journal* article in 2013 entitled, "The Brains of the Animal Kingdom," in which he argued that we have grossly misunderstood animal intelligence:

> It is quite puzzling, therefore, why the field of animal cognition has such a long history of claims about the absence of capacities based on just a few strolls through the forest. Such conclusions contradict the famous dictum of experimental psychology according to which absence of evidence is not evidence of absence.
>
> Take the question of whether we are the only species to care about the well-being of others. It is well known that apes in the wild offer spontaneous assistance to each other, defending against leopards, say, or consoling distressed companions with tender embraces. But for decades, these observations were ignored, and more attention was paid to experiments according to which the apes were entirely selfish. They had been tested with an apparatus to see if one chimpanzee was willing to push food toward another. But perhaps the apes failed to understand the apparatus. When we instead used a simple choice between tokens they could exchange for food—one kind of token rewarded only the chooser, the other kind rewarded both apes—lo and behold, they preferred outcomes that rewarded both of them.
>
> Such generosity, moreover, may not be restricted to apes. In a recent study, rats freed a trapped companion even when a container with chocolate had been put right next to it. Many rats first liberated the other, after which both rodents happily shared the treat.

The one historical constant in my field is that each time a claim of human uniqueness bites the dust, other claims quickly take its place. Meanwhile, science keeps chipping away at the wall that separates us from the other animals. We have moved from viewing animals as instinct-driven stimulus-response machines to seeing them as sophisticated decision makers.

Aristotle's ladder of nature is not just being flattened; it is being transformed into a bush with many branches. This is no insult to human superiority. It is long-overdue recognition that intelligent life is not something for us to seek in the outer reaches of space but is abundant right here on earth, under our noses.[123]

We cite de Waal not as an animal rescuer but as a renowned thought leader and primatologist who, like Goodall, Marc Bekoff, and numerous animal conservationists, has shaped our awareness of the nobility and unique gifts of the non-human animal at a moment of unprecedented jeopardy for all living beings on this planet.

Frans de Waal may be contacted at: http://www.emory.edu/LIVING LINKS/people/dewaal.shtml

Marc Bekoff

In 2010, Emeritus Professor of Ecology and Evolutionary Biology at the University of Colorado, Marc Bekoff, published his *Animal Manifesto*, in which he asserted that:

- All animals share the Earth and we must coexist.
- Animals think and feel.
- Animals have and deserve compassion.
- Connection breeds caring, alienation breeds disrespect.
- Our world is not compassionate to animals.
- Acting compassionately helps all beings and our world.

Why such a manifesto? In the author's own words when we interviewed him:

> Animals are constantly asking us in their own ways to treat them better or leave them alone. This book is their manifesto. In it, I explain what they want and need from us and why they are fully justified in making these requests. We must stop ignoring their gaze and closing our hearts to their pleas. We can easily do what they ask—to stop causing them unnecessary pain, suffering, loneliness, sadness, and death, even extinction. It's a matter of making different choices: about how we conduct research to learn about the natural world and to develop human medicine, about how we entertain ourselves, about what we buy, where we live, who we eat, who we wear, and even family planning. Please join me. The animals need us, and just as importantly, we need them. This manifesto presents a much-needed revolution—a paradigm shift in what we feel and what we do regarding animals—that has to happen now because the current paradigm doesn't work. The status quo has wreaked havoc on animals and Earth. Denial and apathy must be replaced by urgency. If we all work to improve the lives of animals, we will improve our lives as well.[124]

In a conversation with Bekoff who lives in Carolyn's hometown of Boulder, Colorado, he expressed optimism about the increase in laws against animal abuse in the United States, and while admittedly, many are weak, others are quite substantial and are strictly enforced. In terms of bans on the ivory trade in certain nations, Bekoff notes that it is easier to "ban things" as opposed to making them illegal. Enforcement of existing laws is the key rather than the creation of more laws.

In terms of trophy hunting, there are virtually no laws. In fact, according to Bekoff, the industry is so lucrative on so many levels that its profitability is comparable only to drug trafficking, which raises the question of the extent to which drug money is involved. Trophy hunters argue that their hunting is actually serving the poor human inhabitants of the hunting area whose livestock may be at risk of being devoured by a wild animal. However, killing the wild animal reveals a lack of willingness to seriously explore other options.

Similarly, we suffer a failure of imagination when contemplating the horrors of industrial agriculture, sometimes called "factory farming." As Bekoff points out, almost no farming is occurring because the animals are treated like widgets—born into horrible suffering where they endure until they are slaughtered. Bekoff advocates the immediate cessation of factory farming and the release of all animals in its captivity. Predictably, the immediate question asked by those who lack imagination or the willingness to explore options is: "What in the world will we do with all of those animals?" Another dilemma which humans could resolve if they wanted to.

Education is key. What few laws and regulations we have now are the result of education in the past. Bekoff emphasizes that what matters in terms of alleviating animal suffering is not taking into account how "smart" they are, but understanding the emotional lives of animals and the fact that they feel pain profoundly. In fact, studies on rodents have revealed that they are far more intelligent than we have assumed, yet 90 percent of animal research subjects are rodents. Bekoff argues that regardless of what new laws and regulations arise and even how strictly they are enforced, they may be much less effective than education in creating meaningful change in terms of how humans treat animals.

Marc Bekoff may be contacted at: http://marcbekoff.com/

LINDA TUCKER and JASON A. TURNER:
The Global White Lion Protection Trust

As we noted in the introduction to this book, half of the lion trophies coming out of Africa are shot by American hunters. One of the most astonishing "she/roes" of animal conservation is Linda Tucker who has committed her life to protecting white lions. A rare variant of the African lion (*Panthera leo krugeri*), white lions are found in only one place on Earth — the Greater Timbavati-Kruger National Park region of South Africa. The lions are gravely endangered, but seven of these majestic animals roam free in their ancestral heartlands today thanks to the Global White Lion

Protection Trust that Tucker helped set up in 2002. The trust manages the Tsau White Lion Heartland, a protected wilderness area, and also works to protect the Indigenous Tsonga and Sepedi people and cultures that celebrate the white lion as part of their sacred heritage.

Tucker is a former model and ad executive who grew up in South Africa during the Apartheid. Her book, *Saving the White Lions: One Woman's Battle for Africa's Most Sacred Animal* is written in first-person narrative style, telling the story of Tucker's incredible, almost surreal, journey into the world of big wildlife conservation, her struggles to protect the lions against the notorious canned trophy hunting industry, unscrupulous zoo executives, and commercial traders that regard these rare animals as high-income commodities. *Saving the White Lions* is also, in part, a book about Tucker's own spiritual growth starting from the night when a local medicine woman walked out of the wilderness and rescued her and a group of friends from an angry pride of lions. One of the most mystical stories in the book has to do with the birth of a white lion cub called Marah on December 25, 2000, in a trophy-hunting facility in the little South African town of Bethlehem.

We spoke with Linda's partner, Jason A. Turner, specialist lion ecologist, and asked him what is being done in Africa to save wildlife and curb trophy hunting and poaching. We also discussed the devastating effects of climate chaos on the environment of South Africa.

As will be shown below, Jason tells us that all wildlife in Africa is in crisis. Legislation and policy in African countries is not protecting wildlife, making it open to exploitation and driving all species towards extinction. Conservation policies are focused on 'sustainable utilization', which is fine in theory, but unfortunately is open to extreme exploitation due to the lack of law enforcement, and high levels of corruption typical of most African countries. Public pressure through mass media campaigns is putting pressure on African governments to improve conservation policy and legislation; for example the CECIL campaign, named after Cecil the lion, which went viral via social media platforms. In a South African context, independent non-governmental organizations and non-profit conservation organizations such as the Global White Lion Protection Trust (GWLPT), Blood Lions, International Wildlife Bond, Endangered Wildlife Trust, Born Free Foundation, and Campaign Against Canned Hunting, are exposing the failure of the South African conservation authority, the Department of Environmental Affairs, in terms of their conservation policy, having allowed the continuation of the heinous canned hunting industry, and having legalized the lion bone trade in 2017, which is already leading to an increase in poaching of wild lions for local traditional medicine as well as for trade to the Far East, and most especially Laos.[125] Wildlife trafficking in Africa has been identified as the fastest growing money-making industry and includes trade in every imaginable species either for live trade or for their parts such as lion bones, rhino horns, pangolin scales, shark fins, elephant tusks, mountain gorilla and chimpanzee parts, live trade in African rock python, and even leopard tortoise.

On the ground there is an unprecedented mobilization of anti-poaching efforts – both from South African National Parks, private game reserves, and independent game farms in South Africa – in an attempt to counter the poaching of rhinoceros and lions, for their horn and parts, and all game species for the live trade or the bush meat trade. But one of the biggest challenges is how well-organized the poaching syndicates are (militarily trained and well-equipped in terms of weapons), and the high incidence and risk of insider involvement, due to the pay-off being offered to anti-poaching rangers and conservation officials to assist poachers. Highly trained tracker dogs are also crucial in the battle against wildlife poaching; dogs that are trained to locate and apprehend poachers, and are also able to locate snares (traps) or carcass remains from poached animals. Innovative technology is also being used: (1) drones (Unmanned Aerial Vehicles) with specialized cameras to cover vast areas to locate poachers, (2) radio isotopes impregnated in animal parts (such as the rhino horn) as a forensic tool to identify poached animals and illegal trade.

We then asked Jason what must be done going forward to spare and protect wildlife in Africa? We know that Linda and Jason are most familiar with these issues in terms of the white lion, but we wanted to see a broader perspective if possible. Jason told us that in terms of lion conservation, the solution is a multi-pronged one. Governments need to rewrite policy to better protect lions (and all wildlife). Canned hunting (hunting of captive bred lions in small areas) and the lion bone trade needs to be banned. Fundamental to saving species from extinction is that local rural communities become stakeholders in the protection of wildlife and the natural environment, so that they recognize the importance of conserving their natural heritage. In this regard the work being done by Linda Tucker and the GWLPT is critical. The white lion has cultural significance to local Sepedi and Tsonga communities, such that they recognize that to protect the white lion, their prey and natural habitat also have to be protected. The white lion is therefore an important capstone animal for protecting the entire lion population in the Greater Kruger National Park Region of South Africa, one of only 10 viable lion populations that still exist in Africa which is recognized by UNESCO as the third-largest biosphere region in the world: Kruger to Canyon Biosphere. A similar conservation model exists in British Columbia, Canada with the Spirit Bear / Kermode Bear (*Ursus americanus kermodei*) which is a natural color form of the black bear that is revered by the First Nation Kitasoo people, and is thus protected by law by the Canadian government. 220 000 hectares has been given for their protection, and they are a flagship for protecting 4, 000 000 hectares of wilderness in the Great Bear Rainforest. Since there are similar totem animals all over the world, this model is replicable and fundamental to the solution to protecting wildlife globally.

Linda and Jason may be contacted at: https://whitelions.org/

Susan Eirich: Earthfire Institute

On a quiet Saturday morning in April, 2018, Carolyn had an online conversation with Susan Eirich, founder of Earthfire Institute and Wild Animal Sanctuary in Idaho. They talked in undisrupted calm until after a few minutes of conversation, a piercing wolf howl in response to the presence of a nearby coyote accompanied them for a few more minutes. Nothing could have been more appropriate than this unsolicited serenade, highlighting the story Susan shared with Carolyn regarding the origins of Earthfire and her work.

"It was all the fault of seven wolf puppies," said Susan. "I was invited to help care for them. Bottle feeding them, nursing them when they fell desperately ill, I fell in love. That changed everything. It was the kind of passionate, committed love that a parent feels for a newborn child.

"I was helpless before it. I had to do right by them. Then, because they opened me to the wonder of wolves, I had to do right by their kind. As I was invited to care for bears, cougars, lynx, bison, deer and more, I found myself falling in love each time anew! My feelings responded of their own volition. Bemused, I would watch them rising from within, surprised at their intensity. From where did they come? I was falling in love with so many different creatures, so different from my own species. What was the common ground that my body recognized?

"As my awareness expanded, I realized I had to do right by all Life. Falling in love deeply opens channels through which all kinds of information can flow and I saw each living being, plant, tree, animal, as a source of wonder if only I was able to connect with each on its own terms."

As a friend later told Susan, "You know what happened to you Susan? You experienced motherhood."

Susan continued, "Once I was touched by it, saw it, felt it, then I had to fight for the beloved, protect it, take action. If I didn't, it felt like I would have betrayed my very soul. I had to share with others who these beings were, and I had to do something about how we treat wolves. My urge was not so much to *save* them, but to share their beauty and ask, 'Why are we treating them this way? What would we humans be like if we felt them, opened to them, loved them, and truly saw not only their beauty, but what they can teach us?' It's my job to help fellow-humans see."

In 2000 Susan founded Earthfire Institute Wildlife Sanctuary, a multi-species endeavor. It has been a profound and difficult joyous journey since then, which continues; each day, week, year is a delight, a trouble and an amazement. An ever-increasing awakening. A microcosm, she believes, of our human journey.

But really the story of Earthfire is simply a story of love.

Currently, Susan is doing everything possible to share who these beings are and to bring people in and help engage them with animals in order to empower them. She also attempts to teach people how to live with less, which helps all living beings on the planet. She holds the space so that people can hear the call of how they need to engage. She also teaches people to love and save the land and pay very close attention to what they use. Nothing is to be wasted; nothing is to be taken for granted. When you see what is, you just naturally want to take care of it.

As Susan looks at the state of animals on Earth, she feels that the animals are urgently asking us to connect, perhaps more forwardly than they ever have. More people are wanting to connect and understanding what's missing. The more we can listen, the more potential for a shift in our consciousness and in the well-being of human and all animals.

Susan noted that one very powerfully destructive factor is the international criminal gang and corporate elements involved in animal abuse: Drug trafficking, poaching, trophy hunting, dog fighting, factory farming, and other highly lucrative horrors of animal extermination. This is why people must gain their own personal power in order to counterbalance these enormously predatory powers. She (and we) believe that's beginning to happen.

The main ray of hope is the shift in listening. We're seeing baby steps such as an increase in people including dogs in their lives—allowing them to take plane trips with us, incorporating them in hospitals and nursing homes, using comfort dogs in stressful situations. The next step is to include wild animals in our lives in a way that enlarges our sense of the Earth community. This is the place from which we must make decisions, and if we made decisions from that place, says Susan, we would have no environmental problems.

The *ache of the beauty of animals,* and having it be unseen, is a profound motivator for Susan. Carolyn was stunned and stopped by this statement and needed to mull, "the ache of the beauty and having it be unseen," for days after their conversation. We ache along with Susan as we witness the incredible obtuseness of our species toward not only the beauty but the intelligence and wisdom that animals offer us.

Susan speaks of heartbreak and how important it is to be there for animals any way, especially when they are suffering or dying. We humans have only begun to understand the power of connection—and the power of disconnection. What comes from both becomes so elaborate and so enormous, yet it is so simple. The fundamental positions are: Us and them—or us. And everything flows from the choice of those positions.

Susan may be contacted at: http://earthfireinstitute.org/

Linda Bender: Animal Wisdom

We interviewed veterinarian Linda Bender, author of *Animal Wisdom: Learning from the Spiritual Lives of Animals*, who has become an activist on behalf of animals. She very astutely observes that, "Animals' own suffering has made them aware of human suffering. More frequent contact with us has sensitized them to what troubles us. They feel our anxiety and our confusion and, most of all, our loneliness. The pain of being disconnected from the Earth, from each other, from our fellow creatures, and from the Source of all life is the worst pain they can imagine, and they are concerned about us. They understand even better than we do that the suffering we inflict on them is an expression of our own suffering, and that their physical situation cannot get better unless the human spiritual condition gets better. They want to help."[126] In other words, according to Linda, the other-than-human world is well aware of the tortured human animal.

In her opinion, the Trump Administration has declared full-on war on the natural world. When people tell her that they don't want anything to do with politics, she responds with, "That's over." Because as she travels domestically and globally, she sees that people are now stepping forward and getting involved themselves rather than relying on experts to take action.

She's noticing that education and awareness of animal suffering is changing attitudes, sometimes even very early in life. She notes a Cambridge University study "Pets Are a Child's Best Friend, Not Their Siblings" which concludes that, "The research adds to increasing evidence that household pets may have a major influence on child development, and could have a positive impact on children's social skills and emotional well-being." Just as the abuse of animals is a significant predictor of mistreatment of other humans later in life, developing a loving relationship with a household pet may be a predictor of companionship and disclosure in human relationships.[127]

Shortly before our interview Linda had spent six weeks in contemplation about animals and the state of the world. Her sense was that if animals could speak to us, they would say, "You think you have lots of problems, but you really only have one big problem: You think you're separate."

"This is a time of experience," says Linda, and in her contemplation she received a profound message from her deeper Self: "Live in this world in peace with your brothers and sisters in harmony with all life—know this, live this."

Linda may be contacted at: http://lindabender.org/

Lyn White: Animals Australia

Lyn White is the Director of Strategy for Animals Australia. She is recognized and respected as one of Australia's foremost animal advocates and animal cruelty investigators.

A former police officer, Lyn spent much of her early career fighting on behalf of human victims, but it is for her work as an animal advocate that she has been honored as a *Member of the Order of Australia* (AM), named one of Australia's most influential women, and a two-time state finalist for *Australian of the Year.*

After 20 years in the South Australian Police Force, a chance reading of a magazine article about bear bile farming set Lyn on the path to animal advocacy. She worked with the Animals Asia Foundation on animal cruelty issues in South East Asia before joining Animals Australia in 2003.

Lyn's investigations since then into Australia's live export trade have provided the Australian public, livestock producers, and politicians an insight into the brutal treatment of Australian animals sent overseas for slaughter. Evidence gathered over 11 years in 16 countries has resulted in significant industry reform. Under Lyn's guidance, Animals Australia investigators continue to provide the only independent oversight of the live trade in importing countries.

As Animals Australia's Strategic Director, Lyn spearheaded strategic public awareness initiatives to shine a spotlight on the treatment of animals raised for food in factory farms, on dogs abused in the puppy factory trade, and more recently headed investigations exposing shocking cruelty in Australia's greyhound racing industry.

Lyn is also the Director of Animals International, the global arm of Animals Australia, collaborating with international colleague groups on universal animal cruelty issues from factory farming to live export. Her work has led to unprecedented animal welfare advancements in a number of countries, including in Jordan where she serves as Chief Adviser to the Princess Alia Foundation.

Lyn's life experiences are unique and provide an insight into the systems of justice in place for humans and animals. She presents a compelling argument that the causes of human and animal suffering are the same—and that we cannot address one without addressing the essence of both. Moreover she deeply challenges the essence of our humanity by advocating that we are not simply here to be human beings, but to become *humane* beings—and to leave this world a kinder and more compassionate place for those who follow us.

The importance of Lyn's work has received critical international acclaim.

- "Lyn's ethos embodies the line from The Impossible Dream, 'to be willing to march into hell for a Heavenly cause.' She has done this time and again, and thank God, has been rewarded with truly beneficial and far-reaching results for animals and humanity. I am simply in awe of her."—*HRH Princess Alia al Hussein of Jordan*

- "In my forty years working with various organizations to reduce the needless suffering of both humans and animals, I have never known someone as brave and resolute—or as effective as Lyn. Lyn's work has already prevented a vast amount of cruelty, and I am sure that in the future it will prevent much more. Lyn seems to me to have exactly the qualities that Australians look for in their heroes: a quiet no-nonsense get-the-job-done approach, combined with compassion for the weak and an abhorrence of cruelty."—*Professor Peter Singer, University Centre for Human Values*

Lyn is an accomplished public speaker and has undertaken two national tours, speaking to sell-out audiences in capital cities across Australia about how our treatment of animals challenges the finest elements of our humanity.

As Australia's most recognizable animal advocate, her work keeps her in the headlines, however, Lyn much prefers life out of the spotlight. In the rare moments of quiet she will be enjoying long walks with her adopted border collie, Buddy, on the beaches of Victoria's Mornington Peninsula, where she currently resides.[128]

Gene Baur: Farm Sanctuary

An organization dear to our hearts is Farm Sanctuary with three shelters for farm animals in the United States: Upstate New York, Southern California, and Northern California. According to the Farm Sanctuary website:

> *Factory farms dominate U.S. food production, employing abusive practices that maximize agribusiness profits at the expense of the environment, our communities, animal welfare, and even our health.*
>
> *Far from the idyllic, spacious pastures that are shown in advertisements for meat, milk, and eggs, factory farms typically consist of large numbers of animals being raised in extreme confinement. Animals on factory farms are regarded as commodities to be exploited for profit. They undergo painful mutilations and are bred to grow unnaturally fast and large for the purpose of maximizing meat, egg, and milk production for the food industry. Their bodies cannot support this growth, which results in debilitating and painful conditions and deformities.*
>
> *The factory farming industry puts incredible strain on our natural resources. The extreme amount of waste created by raising so many animals in one place pollutes our land, air, and water. Residents of rural communities surrounding factory farms report high incidents of illness, and their property values are often lowered by their proximity to industrial farms. To counteract the health challenges presented by overcrowded, stressful, unsanitary living conditions, antibiotics are used extensively on factory farms, which can create drug-resistant bacteria and put human health at risk.[129]*

Gene Baur, founder of Farm Sanctuary, has been hailed as "the conscience of the food movement" by *Time* magazine. Since the mid-1980s, he has traveled extensively, campaigning to raise awareness about the abuses of industrialized factory farming and our system of cheap food production.

A pioneer in the field of undercover investigations and farm animal rescue, Gene has visited hundreds of farms, stockyards, and slaughterhouses, documenting the deplorable conditions. His pictures and videos exposing factory farming cruelties have aired nationally and internationally, educating millions about the plight of modern farm animals, and his rescue work inspired an international farm sanctuary movement.

Gene has also testified in courts and before local, state, and federal legislative bodies, advocating for better conditions for farm animals. His most important achievements include winning the first-ever cruelty conviction at a U.S. stockyard and introducing the first U.S. laws to prohibit cruel farming confinement methods in Florida, Arizona, and California. His efforts have been covered by top news organizations, including *The New York Times, Los Angeles Times, Chicago Tribune*, and *The Wall Street Journal*. Gene has published two bestsellers, *Farm Sanctuary: Changing Hearts and Minds About Animals and Food* (Scribner, 2008) and *Living the Farm Sanctuary Life* (Rodale, 2015), which he co-authored with *Forks Over Knives* author Gene Stone. Through his writing and his international speaking engagements, Gene provides simple actionable solutions coupled with a compassion-first approach to help us be the change we wish to see in treatment toward animals and in our food system.[130]

Farm Sanctuary rescues, rehabilitates, and provides lifelong care for hundreds of animals who have been saved from stockyards, factory farms, and slaughterhouses. At their three shelters, rescued residents are given the care and love they need to recover from abuse and neglect. All of the animals enjoy nourishing food, clean barns, and green pastures each and every day.

According to Farm Sanctuary:

> Undercover investigations show pigs and other farm animals, who are sick or disabled by the cruelty of factory farming, being beaten, dragged by their ears or tails, pushed with

forklifts, and shocked with electric prods to get them onto the kill floor so they can be slaughtered for profit.

When President Obama took office, he announced a rule banning the slaughter of adult cattle who are too sick or injured to walk. But this victory left other farm animals unprotected. Farm Sanctuary responded with a regulatory petition to the USDA to extend the rule to all livestock, including pigs. Unfortunately, their petition was temporarily rejected.

But we are not giving up this fight, and we have rallied a coalition of eight national animal protection groups to demand an end to the slaughter of the hundreds of thousands of crippled pigs who arrive for slaughter every year.[131]

Farm Sanctuary is organizing and petitioning for laws regulating the slaughter of sick animals and poultry, laws against the use of antibiotics in animals, laws against the slaughter of horses, the performing of surgeries on animals by workers who are untrained in veterinary or surgical skills, and the outright merciless abuse and torture of farm animals for human pleasure.

Farm Sanctuary also conducts massive education projects online and in person to expand understanding regarding the suffering of farm animals and what humans can do to alleviate it.

Farm Sanctuary may be contacted at: https://www.farmsanctuary.org/

Jill Angelo Birnbaum: The Moon Dog Farm

Jill Angelo is a beautiful fifty-year old woman, who looks fifteen years younger. She is immensely direct, passionate, laser-focused, and committed with her whole being to the service and welfare of animals of all kinds. She has been Andrew's executive director of the Institute of Sacred Activism since its creation eight years ago. Andrew writes, "Jill is the most authentic sacred activist I know. I rely absolutely on her fierce integrity, honesty, and strategic brilliance. Without her at my side, without her grounding encouragement, unwavering loyalty, and hands-on example, the Institute would not exist and my work and life would have been much harder and more lonely. She is also one of my most trusted friends."

Jill lives on 1.25 acres in a snug fixer-upper farmhouse in rural Illinois. With her husband Scott, she has turned that property into The Moon Dog Farm, a sanctuary for battered, sick and abandoned dogs. Besides working with Andrew and other spiritual teachers, she works as a consultant for Unity Books and as a server in a local restaurant.

Andrew interviewed her on a recent wintery Chicago morning.

A: You often say your home in Illinois gives you strength and peace. After being a city girl for so long, you now live on your land with thirty old oak trees, deer, hawks, owls, blue jays, cardinals, three garden snakes.

J: Don't forget the salamanders, chipmunks, squirrels, and doves! Before I moved here I had no idea how nourishing country life can be. A calm, steady, buoyant energy flows to me always from this beautiful land. However stressed I sometimes get—you know how grueling working with animals can be—whenever I step out on my porch and look out onto this simple peace of ordinary heaven, I feel blessed to live here with my dogs, guinea pigs, rabbits, and Skitty the cat, my anxiety leaves me. There's something in this land that says to me, "anxiety is not allowed here!"

A: How do you account for your love of animals?

J: I came from a normally dysfunctional middle-class family. I'm the daughter of a cop and a mother who worked most of her life in retail. From early on animals were my best friends. I could trust them in a way I couldn't trust humans. I felt unconditional love from them. They didn't care about my grades or the way I looked. As a cop's daughter I have an innately suspicious nature. Animals didn't make me suspicious; their motives were obvious and pure.

High school was the hardest part of my life. I was awkward, tiny, and wore braces. Although I was very outspoken and seemed to be popular, I secretly felt insecure. Although I had many human friends, animals were my true friends; I could be myself with them. Often my passion can be misunderstood for anger and my force-of-nature personality misinterpreted as controlling. Animals see, feel, and know me as I am.

My first dog was a Samoyed named Chynna. In many ways she was a mirror image of me: determined, playful, independent, and loving—and she broke down all the walls I had put up as a child and adolescent. As I speak to you now, I realize it was Chynna who began the passion I have to help animals.

A: One of the things I admire about you is that you've always been, as long as I've known you, fearless in your confrontation of suffering. You've known heartbreak and tragedy not just through working with animals, but also in your own personal life. Your fiancé was killed in a car crash when you were thirty-two.

J: One thing I believe deeply: suffering is inevitable in life. It comes to everyone, sooner or later. Resisting it is futile. Why swim upstream? Hearts are made to break and heartbreak can make you passionate to serve and help what breaks your heart.

As my love of animals grew, I came to learn more about the dreadful circumstances so many animals suffer. Two years ago I decided I had to do something more than just love and look after my own dogs. I had to start a sanctuary. So I persuaded my husband to move out here and begin The Moon Dog Farm.

A: Scott supported you from the first?

J: Scott loves animals, but it was my passion and dream to buy this land forty-five minutes outside Chicago and start this sanctuary. It amazes me constantly how selflessly and tenderly Scott supports me. We work as a team. He makes me feel that with support like his, the possibilities are endless. He doesn't just support me; he works every day with me to fulfill the next level of our dream for TMDF. I come up with the vision; his steady pragmatic mind comes up with shrewd ways to realize it.

Let me tell you a story about the kind of man I've been blessed with. We took in an unadoptable hamster whose head touches his shoulder. Scott not only welcomed him, he cleared a space for him on his own dresser and bought him a ball. That says it all.

A: Tell me about the schedule of your day?

J: Scott and I get up between 5:00 and 6:00 every morning. Then we feed our pack of resident dogs. They have to go out and do their business. After they return and get settled, we turn to the three foster dogs we currently have with us, and we dispense medications as needed. When they are settled, we deal with our house rabbit, our foster rabbit, our house guinea pig, and two foster guinea pigs whose cages and bedding are cleaned every day and who need to be given fresh hay, food and water. Then we go into our climate-controlled garage where we've made what I call a palace—a 12 X 4 foot enclosure—in which we keep a 14-pound male Lop rabbit named Freddy, and Daisy May, a 17-pound Flemish giant rabbit and tend to them.

By the time we've done all this, it is time to let the dogs out again. Playtime is at 11:00 AM for about an hour. From 7:00 AM onward, I have my phone on to deal with the immediate needs of any of my clients, and between noon and 3:00 PM I get to my desk to do the urgent business that's needed that day. Then it's time to let the dogs out yet again. They eat at 4:30 PM, go out again at 7 PM, and we play with them for about an hour. By 10 at night, Scott and I are in bed. Our date nights are usually going grocery shopping and catching a quick early bite at 4:30 or 5 PM. We never leave our animals for more than four hours and if we have to, we always get someone in. I couldn't live with myself if anything happened to any one of them.

As you can see, everything we both do in our day revolves around our animals. Some of my old friends who knew me in a different life call this a sacrifice. I don't. I am doing what I most love and believe in with a man I love, who loves and supports me in a place that brings me healing and peace. I've traveled a great deal and had a lot of perks. The traveling was great, but I came to realize the corporate life wasn't my calling. I'm the happiest and fullest I've ever been. Living your passion will do that for you.

A: What is your vision for The Moon Dog Farm?

J: I would love to expand it, by buying nearby land and getting enough donations to hire an assistant I could trust completely. I would like also to inspire other animal lovers to do what Scott and I do. Animals all over the world are suffering horribly in our deepening world crisis. You don't have to be rich to help, just willing to step up. My daily prayer is that TMDF will inspire others just like Scott and me—ordinary hard-working people who put their love and concern for animals into real hands-on action and create simple oases and sanctuaries where animals can feel respected, loved, and looked after. In the two years we've been doing this, the response has been extraordinary, beyond my wildest dreams. And I'm happy to say it is growing.

A: What advice would you offer to those reading this?

J: Best of all, adopt an animal. If you can't adopt, foster. If you can't foster, sponsor. If you can't sponsor, volunteer. If you can't volunteer, donate. If you can't donate, educate. Don't ever tell me you can't help! There is always something you can do. Given what is now happening to animals everywhere, help is desperately needed—more than ever.

Jill may be contacted at http://www.themoondogfarm.com/

We pray that this book has been a genuine initiation for you. We trust that its musical structure has awoken in you both a vision of what humanity can be when it returns to the embrace of the creation and what has to be transmuted in all of us in order to make this possible. The goal of an initiation is not only, however, expanded consciousness. It is to put that consciousness into action. What action will you take?

A Prayer by Albert Schweitzer

Hear our humble prayer, O God, for our friends the animals,
especially for animals who are suffering;
for animals that are overworked, underfed and cruelly
treated;
for all wistful creatures in captivity that beat their wings
against bars;
for any that are hunted or lost or deserted or frightened or
hungry;
for all that must be put death.
We entreat for them all Thy mercy and pity,
and for those who deal with them we ask a heart of
compassion
and gentle hands and kindly words.
Make us, ourselves, to be true friends to animals,
and so to share the blessings of the merciful.[132]

APPENDIX

One question we are often asked is if we are vegans. We honor the vegan movement and deeply respect the reasons for veganism. We have been alarmed, however, by the tendency some vegans have toward what can only be called fundamentalism. This dangerously limits their appeal and also prevents those who resist this fundamentalism from entering into a deep communion with animals. As one animal-loving friend who is a vegetarian said to Andrew after listening with him to one of the world's most passionate advocates of veganism, "All I want to do now is to go out and have a bloody steak. Of course I won't, but I understand why anyone would." Shaming people around veganism will never be productive. Living a vegan lifestyle with grace and compassion toward others who do not share that lifestyle will have over time a far greater impact.

We find great and sobering wisdom in the following commentary by Derrick Jensen, one of our greatest living champions of a new relationship with the creation. In his indispensable masterpiece, *The Myth of Human Superiority*, he writes:

> Sometimes, because I eat meat (that doesn't come from factory farms), vegans have accused me of *speciesism*. But the truth is quite the opposite. I don't believe in the Great Chain of Being. I believe that plants are every bit as sentient as anyone else. Human supremacists draw the line of being/not-being between humans and nonhumans, with humans being sentient and having lives worth moral (and other) consideration, and nonhuman animals, not so much. Vegans often draw the line of being/not-being between nonhuman animals and plants, with nonhuman animals being (to

varying degrees) sentient and having lives worth moral (and other) consideration, and plants, not so much. I don't see it that way. I believe that no matter whom you eat, you are eating someone.[133]

Suggested Reading List

- *The Sacred White Animals of Prophecy*, Scott Alexander King
- *Kinship With All Life*, J. Allen Boone
- *My Life Among the Underdogs*, Tia Maria Torres
- *Dominion: the Power of Man, the Suffering of Animals, and the Call to Mercy*, Matthew Scully
- *The Myth of Human Superiority*, Derrick Jensen
- *Saving the White Lions: One Woman's Battle for Africa's Most Sacred Animal*, Linda Tucker
- *What the Animals Taught Me*, Stephanie Marohn
- *Second Nature: The Inner Lives of Animals*, Johnathan Balcombe
- *Are We Smart Enough to Know How Smart Animals Are?* Frans de Waal
- *The Animal Manifesto*, Marc Bekoff
- *The Ten Trusts: What We Must Do to Care for the Animals We Love*, Jane Goodall and Marc Bekoff
- *Becoming Animal*, David Abram
- *Fear of the Animal Planet: The Hidden History of Animal Resistance*, Jason Hribal
- *Other Minds*, Peter Godfrey Smith
- *The Soul of an Octopus*, Sy Montgomery
- *Animal Wisdom*, Linda Bender, DVM

Recommended Organizations Saving and Serving Animals

- The Moon Dog Farm, founded and managed by Jill Angelo Birnbaum
  https://www.themoondogfarm.com/about/jill-angelo

- Global White Lion Protection Trust, founded by Linda Tucker and Jason Turner
  https://www.lindatuckerfoundation.org/the-global-white-lion-protection-trust/

- Earthfire Institute, founded and managed by Susan Eirich
  https://earthfireinstitute.org/

- Animals Australia, Investigations Director, Lyn White
  https://www.animalsaustralia.org/

- Farm Sanctuary, Founded and Directed by Gene Baur
  https://www.farmsanctuary.org/

- Villalobos Rescue Center, Founded and Directed by Tia Maria Torres
  http://www.vrcpitbull.com/

- Linda Bender, DVM, Animal Wisdom: Advocating For Animals
  https://lindabender.org/

ENDNOTES

1   Bill Plotkin, *Wild Mind: A Field Guide to the Human Psyche*, New World Library, 2013, p. 7.

2   (Prayer offered at *The Meaning of Life: A Multifaith Consultation, Mauritius, January 25-February 3, 1983*. As cited in <u>*Towards an Intercultural Theology*</u>, 56.)

3   Andrew Harvey, *Light Upon Light: Inspirations from Rumi,* North Atlantic Books, 1996, p. 96.

4   Pirkei Avot, collection of rabbinic sayings, compiled 250–275 CE <u>https://en.wikipedia.org/wiki/Pirkei_Avot</u>

5   Andrew Harvey, *The Direct Path*, Broadway Books, 2000, pp. 146–149.

6   Andrew Harvey, *Turn Me to Gold: 108 Poems of Kabir*, Unity Books, 2018, p.174.

7   Sylvia Chidi, "The Animal In Me," Poem Hunter, 2006, <u>https://www.poemhunter.com/poem/the-animal-in-me/</u>

8   J. Zohara Meyerhoff Hieronimus, *White Spirit Animals: Prophets of Change* (pp. 9–10). Inner Traditions/Bear & Company, 2017.

9   *Ibid.*, p. 12.

10 *Ibid.*, p. 301.

11 Andrew Harvey, *Light the Flame*, Hay House, 2013, p. 98.

12 Andrew Harvey, *Becoming God*, 2019.

13 Susan Eirich, "Wolf Pup Teaches Feral Wolf Dog About Humans," Earthfire Institute, <u>http://earthfireinstitute.org/story/wolf-pup-teaches-shy-dog-about-humans/</u>

14 Stephanie Marohn, *What the Animals Taught Me*, Hampton Roads, 2012, p. 90–91.

15 Linda Tucker, Marah's Life Story, <u>https://www.lindatuckerfoundation.org/marahs-life-story/</u>

16 The Hopi Snake Dance, <u>https://www.brownielocks.com/snakedance.html</u>

17 Christopher Smart, "My Cat Jeoffry," "In Nomine Patris et Felis," Robert Pinsky, Slate Magazine, October, 2009.

18 Andrew Harvey, *The Direct Path,* pp. 234–237.

19 Bill Plotkin, *Soulcraft: Crossing into the Mysteries of Nature and Psyche*, New World Library, 2010, p. 237.

20 Arthur Edington, *The Philosophy of Physical Science*, Cambridge University Press, 1939, p. 222.

21 Theodore Roszak, *Where the Wasteland Ends*, Doubleday, 1972, p. 405.

22 Ovid, *Metamorphoses* as quoted by Jeffrey St. Clair in "Let Us Now Praise Infamous Animals," Counterpunch, August 3, 2018, https://www.counterpunch.org/2018/08/03/let-us-now-praise-infamous-animals-2/

23 Jonathan Balcombe, *Second Nature: The Inner Lives of Animals*, Palgrave Macmillan, 2010, p. 203.

24 "Let Us Now Praise Infamous Animals," Counterpunch, August 3, 2018 https://www.counterpunch.org/2018/08/03/let-us-now-praise-infamous-animals-2/

25 Theodore Roszak, *Where the Wasteland Ends*, pp. 123–124.

26 *Ibid.*, p. 162.

27 *Ibid.*, p. 181.

28 *Ibid.*, p. 234.

29 William Blake, "Pentecost" poem, https://www.poemhunter.com/william-blake/poems/page-1/?a=a&l=3&y=

30 *Ibid.*, p. 395.

31 Frans de Waal, *Bonobo: The Forgotten Ape*, University of California Press, 1997, p. 1.

32 George Page, *Inside the Animal Mind*, Broadway Books, 2001, p. 27.

33 *Ibid.*, p. 42.

34 *Ibid.*, p. 56.

35 Chandogya Upanishad, https://en.wikipedia.org/wiki/Chandogya_Upanishad

36 George Page, *Inside the Animal Mind*, p. 318.

37 *Ibid.*, p. 329.

38 *Ibid.*, p. 354.

39 Daniel Dennett, *Kinds of Minds: Toward an Understanding of Consciousness*, Basic Books, 1996, p. 22.

40 *Ibid.*, p. 167.

41 Frans de Waal, *Are We Smart Enough to Know How Smart Animals Are?*, W. W. Norton, 2017, p. 11.

42 *Ibid.*, p. 52.

43 "More Than Half Your Body Is Not Human," James Gallagher, BBC Online, April 10, 2018, http://www.bbc.com/news/health-43674270

44 Frans de Waal, *Are We Smart Enough to Know How Smart Animals Are?*, p. 68.

45 *Ibid.*, p. 156.

46 *Ibid.*, p. 187.

47 *Ibid.*, p. 240.

48 You Tube, "Studying Elephant Communication," February, 2017, https://www.youtube.com/watch?v=nII9yngRuac&t=53s

49 Frans de Waal, *Are We Smart Enough to Know How Smart Animals Are?*, p. 263.

50   Wikipedia, Angelus Silesius, https://en.wikipedia.org/wiki/Angelus_Silesius

51   Oren Lyons Speech to United Nations, 1992, https://faculty.smu.edu/twalker/orenlyo4.htm

52   Eckhart Tolle, *The Power of Now*, Namaste Publishing, 2004, p. 228.

53   "Ants Nurse Wounded Warriors Back to Health," Phys.Org, February 14, 2018, https://phys.org/news/2018-02-ants-nurse-wounded-warriors-health.html

54   Linda Star Wolf, *Spirit of the Wolf*, Sterling Ethos, 2012.

55   Barry Lopez, *Of Wolves and Men*, Scribner, 1978, p. 87.

56   *Ibid.*, pp. 104–105.

57   *Ibid.*, p. 112.

58   *Ibid.*, p. 140.

59   *Ibid.*, p. 142.

60   Stephanie Marohn, *What the Animals Taught Me*, Hampton Roads, 2012, p. 43.

61   *Ibid.*, pp. 90–91

62   "Scientific Heretic Rupert Sheldrake on Morphic Fields, Psychic Dogs and Other Mysteries," Scientific American, July, 2014, https://blogs.scientificamerican.com/cross-check/scientific-heretic-rupert-sheldrake-on-morphic-fields-psychic-dogs-and-other-mysteries/

63   *Ibid.*

64   Stephanie Marohn, *What the Animals Taught Me*, p. 176.

65   Diane Knoll, *Mysticism and Whales*, Create Space, 2017, p. 39.

66   Thomas Berry, *Dreamer of the Earth: The Spiritual Ecology of the Father of Environmentalism*, Simon & Schuster Digital Edition, 2011, p. 43.

67   Diane Knoll, *Mysticism and Whales*, p. 45.

68   "Imitation of novel conspecific and human speech sounds in the killer whale," Royal Society of Biological Sciences, January 31, 2018, http://rspb.royalsocietypublishing.org/content/285/1871/20172171

69   Diane Knoll, *Mysticism and Whales*, p. 140.

70   Sy Montgomery, *The Soul of an Octopus: A Surprising Exploration into the Wonder of Consciousness*, Atria, 2015, p. 13.

71   Brad Plumer, Vox, https://www.vox.com/2015/11/18/9753832/national-book-award-2015-nominee-reviews

72   Ocean Portal, "How Octopuses and Squids Change Color," http://ocean.si.edu/ocean-news/how-octopuses-and-squids-change-color

73   Mo Costandi, "The Octopus Can See With Its Skin," *Guardian*, May, 2015.

74   Interview with Jane Goodall, https://www.egonzehnder.com/the-focus-magazine/topics/the-focus-on-trust/parallel-worlds/interview-with-primatologist-jane-goodall.html

75   Carl Safina, "Why Anthropomorphism Helps Us Understand Animals' Behavior," Medium, https://medium.com/@carlsafina/why-anthropomorphism-helps-us-understand-animals-behavior-155b69535d17

76 "A Lifetime in the Field," CNN Special Report, January, 2017, https://www.cnn.com/2017/01/17/africa/jane-goodall-conservation/index.html

77 Anuschka de Rohan, "Why Dolphins Are Deep Thinkers," *Guardian,* July, 2003, https://www.theguardian.com/science/2003/jul/03/research.science

78 Stephen T. Newmyer, *Animals, Rights and Reason in Plutarch and Modern Ethics*, Routledge, 2006, p. 83.

79 Lori Marino and Christina Colvin, "Thinking Pigs: A Comparative Review of Cognition, Emotion, and Personality," *Journal of Comparative Psychology,* Vol. 28, 2015.

80 Ferris Jabr, "Elephants Are Even Smarter Than We Realized," *Scientific American,* February, 2014.

81 *Ibid.*

82 Heraclitus, Wikiquote, https://en.wikiquote.org/wiki/Heraclitus

83 Andrew Harvey, *Turn Me to Gold: 1Poems of Kabir,* p. 166.

84 John O'Donohue: *Walking in Wonder,* John O'Donohue Legacy Partnership, 2013, pp. 8–9.

85 Salima Ikram, "Animals in ancient Egyptian religion: belief, identity, power, and economy," Oxford Handbook of Zooarchaeology, 2017.

86 James Hillman, *Animal Presences*, Spring Publications, 2008, p. 181.

87 Rupert Sheldrake, *Dogs That Know When Their Owners Are Coming Home: And Other Unexplained Powers of Animals,* Arrow Publishing, 2000.

88 Rupert Sheldrake, "Listen to the Animals: Why did so many animals escape December's tsunami?" March, 2005, https://www.sheldrake.org/research/animal-powers/listen-to-the-animals

89 Matthew Fox, *Christian Mystics: 3Readings and Meditations*, New World Library, 2011, p. 58.

90 James Hillman, *Animal Presences*, p. 161.

91 *Mirabai: Ecstatic Poems,* "Mira the Barterer," Google Books Online.

92 Marc Bekoff, *The Animal Manifesto*, New World Library, 2010, p. 178.

93 Jason Hribal, *Fear of the Animal Planet*, AK Press, 2011.

94 Henry Beston, *The Outermost House: A Year of Life on the Great Beach of Cape Cod*, Holt Paperbacks, 2003, p. 107.

95 Andrew Harvey, *Essential Mystics: Selections from the World's Great Wisdom Traditions,* Harper One, 1997, p.128.

96 David Abram, *Becoming Animal: An Earthly Cosmology*, Vintage, 10, pp. 4–8.

97 James Hillman, *Animal Presences*, Spring Publications, 2008, pp. 39–40.

98 Ptolemy Tompkins, *The Divine Life of Animals*, Crown Publishers, 2010, p. 50.

99 *Ibid.,* p. 80.

100 *Ibid.,* p. 90–91.

101 *Ibid.,* p. 130.

102 Michigan State University Animal and Legal Historical Center, "The Link: Cruelty to Animals and Violence Toward People," https://www.animallaw.info/article/link-cruelty-animals-and-violence-towards-people

103 Noam Chomsky, Democratic Underground, September, 2008, https://www.democraticunderground.com/discuss/duboard.php?az=view_all&address=389x4043334

104 Derrick Jensen, *The Myth of Human Superiority*, p. 95.

105 Ptolemy Tompkins, *The Divine Life of Animals*, p. 83.

106 Fact Retriever, https://www.factretriever.com/animal-cruelty-facts

107 Jonathan Safran Foer, *Eating Animals*, Little, Brown and Company, 2009.

108 *Ibid.*

109 Kim Masters Evans, *Animal Rights*, Gale Cengage Learning, 2012.

110 *Ibid.*

111 *Ibid.*

112 Karen Dawn, *Thanking the Monkey: Rethinking the Way We Treat Animals*, Harper, 2008.

113 Evans, *Animal Rights*.

114 "Help Stop the Sadistic 'Fire Bull' Festival in Soria." *PETA*, Accessed: February 25, 2013.

115 Humane Society International, http://www.hsi.org/assets/pdfs/report_trophy_hunting_by_the.pdf

116 Faunalytics, https://faunalytics.org/fundamentals-research-animals/?gclid=CjwKCAiA-9rTBRBNEiwAt0Znw7vRfRFnl0QIdOGobf1-lEHRKs7DM3uEAZg8cqwQdNz2TItrWNj0aBoCFRQQAvD_BwE

117 PETA, https://www.peta.org/issues/animals-used-for-experimentation/animals-laboratories/

118 World Wildlife Fund, https://www.worldwildlife.org/press-releases/half-of-global-wildlife-lost-says-new-wwf-report

119 *Guardian*, October 18, 2017, https://www.theguardian.com/environment/2017/oct/18/warning-of-ecological-armageddon-after-dramatic-plunge-in-insect-numbers

120 Animal Underworld: Inside America's Black Market for Rare & Exotic Species, https://www.publishersweekly.com/978-1-891620-28-7

121 Jane Goodall and Marc Bekoff, *The Ten Trusts: What We Must Do to Care for the Animals We Love*, Harper San Francisco, 2002, p. 138.

122 Jane Goodall, Thane Maynard, Gail Hudson, *Hope for the Animals and Their World*, Grand Central Publishing, 2009, p. 161.

123 Frans de Waal, "The Brains of the Animal Kingdom," *Wall Street Journal*, March 22, 2013, https://www.wsj.com/news/articles/SB10001424127887323869604578370574285382756

124 Marc Bekoff, *The Animal Manifesto: Six Reasons for Expanding Our Compassion Footprint*, New World Library, 2010.

125 Williams VL, Loveridge AJ, Newton DJ, Macdonald DW (2017). Questionnaire survey of the pan-African trade in lion body parts. PLoS ONE 12(10): e0187060. https://doi.org/10.1371/journal.pone.0187060

126 Linda Bender, *Animal Wisdom: Learning from the Spiritual Lives of Animals*, North Atlantic, 2014, p. 11.

127 Matt Cassells, "Pets Are a Child's Best Friend, Not Their Siblings," Cambridge University, January, 2017. http://www.cam.ac.uk/research/news/pets-are-a-childs-best-friend-not-their-siblings

128 Lyn White, Animals Australia, https://www.animalsaustralia.org/about/lyn-white.php

129 Farm Sanctuary Website, https://www.farmsanctuary.org/learn/factory-farming/

130 Gene Baur, Farm Sanctuary Website, https://www.farmsanctuary.org/authors/

131 *Ibid.*, https://www.farmsanctuary.org/get-involved/federal-legislation/

132 Prayer by Albert Schweitzer, https://www.beliefnet.com/prayers/multifaith/compassion/prayer-for-animals.aspx#IWmfE0kYkQt1SVsr.99

133 Derrick Jensen, *The Myth of Human Superiority,* Seven Stories Press, 2016, p. 30.

ABOUT THE AUTHORS

ANDREW HARVEY is the author of more than 30 books, including Turn Me To Gold, 108 Poems of Kabir. A Rumi scholar and a dynamic workshop leader, he is the founder of the Institute for Sacred Activism. (www.andrewharvey.net)

CAROLYN BAKER is a retired psychotherapist and currently offers life coaching and spiritual counseling. She is the author of several books including Collapsing Consciously: Transformative Truths for Turbulent Times. (www.carolynbaker.net)

CPSIA information can be obtained
at www.ICGtesting.com
Printed in the USA
FSHW020953251119
64474FS